DAILY DEVOTIONS FOR A

Life of Purpose

365
INSPIRATIONAL READINGS
ON GOD'S LOVE

COMPILED BY JOHN HUDSON TINER

HUMBLECREEK
INSPIRATION FOR LIFE

© 2006 by Barbour Publishing, Inc.

Compiled by John Hudson Tiner. Previously published as *Show Me Your Love*.

ISBN 1-59789-453-2

Published by Humble Creek, P.O. Box 719, Uhrichsville, Ohio 44683

Printed in the United States of America.
5 4 3 2 1

Introduction

The word *purpose*, according to the dictionary, implies something to accomplish or attain. Those who live a life of purpose live according to a settled determination.

But what is the best purpose in life? Many seek money, power, notoriety, or pleasure as their goals. Often, they succeed in their pursuits—but still experience a certain emptiness. Perhaps there's a better purpose in life.

The Bible would indicate that life's greatest purpose is love. "Now these three remain: faith, hope and love," wrote the apostle Paul. "But the greatest of these is love" (1 Corinthians 13:13 NIV).

Love is both something to accomplish—as the goodness we share with the people around us—and something to attain—as the goodness we receive from God, who is Himself love (1 John 4:8). Love is the greatest purpose we could pursue in this life.

This book, *Daily Devotions for a Life of Purpose*, shares an entire year's worth of readings on love. From great Christians like John Bunyan, Charles Spurgeon, William Tyndale, D. L. Moody, Mary Slessor—and approximately three dozen others—these 365 selections celebrate God's love for you while encouraging you to share that love with others.

If you need a worthy purpose in life, consider the pursuit of love. These readings will help show you the way.

The LORD, your God, is in your midst, a warrior who gives victory;
he will rejoice over you with gladness, he will renew you in his love;
he will exult over you with loud singing. Zephaniah 3:17 NRSV

*W*ithout a renewal of faith, Christians are blind to the state of sinners. The truths of the Bible appear like a dream.

But when they enter into a revival, they see things in that strong light which will renew the love of God in their hearts.

So their love to men will be renewed. They will have a longing desire for the salvation of the whole world. They will be in an agony for individuals whom they want to have saved—their friends, relations, enemies. They will not only be urging them to give their hearts to God, but they will carry them to God in the arms of faith, and with strong crying and tears beseech God to have mercy on them and save their souls from endless burnings.

Charles Finney

WHAT IS LOVE?—JANUARY 2

Praise the LORD, O my soul, and forget not all his benefits who forgives
all your sins and heals all your diseases, who redeems your life from the pit
and crowns you with love and compassion. Psalm 103:2–4 NIV

*W*hat is it to love God but to delight in Him, to rejoice in His will, to desire continually to please Him, to seek and find our happiness in Him, and to thirst day and night for a fuller enjoyment of Him?

As to the measure of this love, our Lord has clearly told us, "You shall love the Lord your God with all your heart." But we are not to love or delight in none but Him. He has commanded us to love our neighbor—that is—all people as ourselves. We are to desire and pursue their happiness as sincerely and steadily as our own. We are to love in the strictest sense: to delight in them and to enjoy them. Love in such a way and measure will prepare us for the enjoyment of Him.

John Wesley

JANUARY 3—BEAUTIFUL LOVE

If I speak in the tongues of men and of angels, but have not love,
I am only a resounding gong or a clanging cymbal. 1 Corinthians 13:1 NIV

*E*veryone has asked the great question: What is the supreme good? You have life before you. Once only you can live it. What is the noblest object of desire, the supreme gift to covet?

Paul says, "If I have all faith, so that I can remove mountains, and have not love, I am nothing." Peter says, "Above all things have fervent love among yourselves." Above all things! And John goes farther, "God is love." Christ said, "I will show you a more simple way." If you do one thing, you will do these many things without ever thinking about them. If you love, you will unconsciously fulfill the whole law. Love is the rule for fulfilling all rules.

Henry Drummond

JANUARY 4—LOVE THAT UNDERSTANDS

O Lord, you have examined my heart and know everything about me.
Psalm 139:1 NLT

*T*here are times when severe fever makes us utterly unaware of the presence of our most careful and tender nurses. A child in delirium will cry out in anguish for its mother. The child is being attended with the untold tenderness of a mother's love. Disease has hidden the mother from the child, but it has not hidden the child from the mother. In the same way, it is with our God and us. The darkness of our fears, sorrows, or despairs cannot hide us from God, although it often hides Him from us.

No one else in all the world understands us. Others misinterpret our actions and misjudge our motives. No one makes allowances for our ill health. No one realizes how much we have to contend with. But our heavenly Father knows it all, and His judgment of us takes into account every element, conscious or unconscious, that goes to make up our character and to control our actions. Only an all-comprehending love can be just, and our God is just.

Hannah Whitall Smith

All night long on my bed I looked for the one my heart loves;
I looked for him but did not find him. Song of Songs 3:1 NIV

The betrothed bride has learned to love her lord, and no other companionship than his can satisfy her. His visits may be occasional and may be brief, but they are precious times of enjoyment. Their memory is cherished in the intervals, and their repetition longed for. There is no real satisfaction in his absence, and yet he comes and goes. As the ever-changing tide, her experience is an ebbing and flowing one. It may even be that unrest is the rule, satisfaction the exception. Is there no help for this? Must it always continue so? Has he created these unquenchable longings only to tantalize them? Strange indeed it would be if this were the case.

The Bridegroom is waiting for you all the time. The conditions that prevent His approach are all of your own making. Take the right place before Him, and He will be most ready, most glad to satisfy your deepest longings, to meet, supply your every need.

Hudson Taylor

LOVE CALLS MISSIONARIES—JANUARY 6

These proclaim Christ out of love, knowing that I have been put here
for the defense of the gospel. Philippians 1:16 NRSV

The obstacles to carrying the gospel among the heathen must arise, I think, from either their distance from us, their primitive manner of living, the danger of being killed by them, the difficulty of acquiring the necessaries of life, or the lack of understanding of their languages.

The apostles and their successors went among foreign people. They did not wait for the ancient inhabitants of other realms to be educated before they could be converted to Christianity. Dealing with them provokes no objection to commercial men. We should have as much love to the souls of our fellow sinners as they have for the profits arising from a few otter skins. After all, the uneducated state of the heathen, instead of affording an objection against preaching the gospel to them, ought to furnish an argument for it.

Does not the goodness of the cause, the duties incumbent on us as Christians call upon us to venture all and use every effort for their benefit?

William Carey

JANUARY 7—FUTURE LOVE

Those who sow in tears will reap with songs of joy.
Psalm 126:5 NIV

*I*t seems perfectly reasonable that God should have given us a glimpse of the future, for we are constantly losing some of our friends by death, and the first thought that comes to us is, *Where have they gone?* Then it is that we turn to the Bible, for there is no other book in all the world that can give us the slightest comfort.

Not long ago, I met an old friend, and as I took him by the hand and asked about his family, the tears came trickling down his cheeks as he said, "I haven't any now. I am left here desolate and alone."

Would anyone take from that man the hope that he will meet his dear ones again? No, we need not forget our dear loved ones. But we cling forever to the enduring hope that there will be a time when we can meet unfettered, and be blessed in that land of everlasting suns, where the soul drinks from the living streams of love that roll by God's high throne.

Dwight Lyman Moody

JANUARY 8—LOVE IS A FACT

But God demonstrates his love for us by the fact that Christ died for us
while we were still sinners. Romans 5:8 ISV

A little boy, who had been studying at school about the discovery of America, said to his father one day, "Father, if I had been Columbus, I would not have taken all that trouble to discover America."

"Why, what would you have done?" asked the father.

"Oh," replied the little boy, "I would have just gone to the map and found it."

This little boy did not understand that maps are only pictures of already known places, and that America did not exist because it was on the map, but it could not be on the map until it was already known to exist. Similarly, the Bible is, like the map, a simple statement of facts. When it tells us that God loves us, it is only telling us something that is a fact, and that would not be in the Bible if it had not been already known to be a fact.

Hannah Whitall Smith

"A new command I give you: Love one another.
As I have loved you, so you must love one another." John 13:34 NIV

*E*very spirit acts with freedom and universality according to what it is. It needs no command to live its own life, or be what it is, no more than you need to bid wrath to be wrathful. Therefore, the spirit of love can only love, wherever it is or goes.

As the sparks know no motion but that of flying upwards, whether it be in the darkness of the night or in the light of the day, so the spirit of love is always in the same course. It knows no difference of time, place, or persons, whether it gives or forgives, bears or forbears; it is equally doing its own delightful work. For the spirit of love is its own blessing and happiness because it is the truth and reality of God in the soul; and therefore, it is in the same joy of life everywhere and on every occasion.

William Law

MERCIFUL LOVE—JANUARY 10

Be mindful of your mercy, O LORD, and of your steadfast love,
for they have been from of old. Psalm 25:6 NRSV

*A*dam and Eve had eaten the fruit of which God had commanded them that they should not eat. When arraigned before God, they could not be brought to confess it. How can God, consistently with His justice, possibly forgive them? Yet mercy cries spare the work of Your own hands!

An amazing scene of divine love here opens to our view, which had been from all eternity hid in the heart of God! Although Adam and Eve were unrepentant and did not so much as put up one single petition for pardon, God immediately passed sentence upon the serpent and revealed to them a Savior.

God the Father and God the Son had entered into a covenant concerning the salvation of the elect from all eternity. The first Adam proved false. Therefore, to secure the second covenant from being broken, God put it into the hands of the second Adam, the Lord from heaven. Adam after the fall stood no longer as our representative. He and Eve were only private persons, as we are, and were only to lay hold on the declaration of mercy contained in this promise by faith.

George Whitefield

And they said one to another, Did not our heart burn within us, while he talked with us by the way, and while he opened to us the scriptures? Luke 24:32 KJV

*C*hristians, does it not now stir up your love to remember all the experiences of His love? Does not kindness melt you and the sunshine of divine goodness warm your frozen hearts? What will it do then, when you shall live in love, and have all in Him who is all? Christians, you will be then brimful of love; yet, love as much as you can, you shalt be ten thousand times more beloved.

Were not the arms of the Son of God open upon the cross and an open passage made to His heart by the spear? Will not His arms and heart be open to you in glory? Did not He begin to love before you loved and will not He continue now? And will He not now immeasurably love you as a son, as a perfect saint? He that in love wept over the old Jerusalem when near its ruin, with what love will He rejoice over the new Jerusalem in her glory!

Richard Baxter

JANUARY 12—FATHER LOVE

Praise be to the God and Father of our LORD Jesus Christ, the Father of compassion and the God of all comfort. 2 Corinthians 1:3 NIV

A father loves his child; therefore, whether it is a smile or a rebuke, it is for the good of the child. God's chastening is not to destroy but to reform. God cannot hurt His children, for He is a tenderhearted Father. Will a father seek the ruin of his child, the child that came from himself, that bears his image? All his care and contrivance is for his child. Whom does he settle the inheritance upon, but his child?

God is an everlasting Father. Before we were children, God was our father, and He will be our father to eternity. A father provides for his child while he lives; but if the father dies, then the child may be exposed to injury. But God never ceases to be a father. You who are a believer have a Father who never dies; and if God be your father, all things must work for your good.

Thomas Watson

"Those whom I love I rebuke and discipline. So be earnest, and repent." Revelation 3:19 NIV

*I*t is a very solemn thing to be dearly loved by God. It is a privilege to be coveted. But the person who is so honored occupies a position of great delicacy. The Lord your God is a jealous God, and He is most jealous where He shows most love. If the Lord gives a church a special blessing, He expects more of it—more care of His honor and more zeal for His glory. When He does not find it, what will happen? Because of His very love, He will rebuke it with hard sermons, sharp words, and painful blows to the conscience.

The best remedy for churches in relapse is increased spiritual fellowship with Christ. Christ is outside the church, driven there by her unkindness, but He has not gone far away; He loves His church too much to leave her altogether. He longs to come back, and therefore He waits and knocks at the door.

Charles Haddon Spurgeon

HOPE AND LOVE—JANUARY 14

He rekindles burned-out lives with fresh hope, restoring dignity and respect to their lives.
1 Samuel 2:8 TM

*I*n the three attributes of admiration, hope, and love, a person's personality abides. Gain them, and you win the person! All three attributes must be regarded in permanent union. The quality of each depends upon the presence of all. Strike out one, and you maim the rest. There is an imperfect love in which there is no admiration. There is an imperfect admiration in which there is no love. Perfect love admires, perfect admiration loves, and love and admiration are ever associated with the gracious spirit of hopeful aspiration. These three constitute the very marrow of life—the deep, secret springs of character and conduct. We live by admiration, hope, and love.

Those who are to gain others for the Master must be careful how they live. The detection of inconsistency is fatal to the reception of our message. "I say" may count for little or nothing. "I know" may count for very little more. "I am" is the personification that gives the defense and confirmation to the gospel, and reveals something of a reflected beauty of the glorious lover Himself.

John Henry Jowett

They refused to obey, and were not mindful of the wonders
that you performed among them. Nehemiah 9:17 NRSV

A boy was sick a little time before, and the mother had watched over him so faithfully and tenderly that she had caught his sickness. She had brought him back to health, but she was lying very sick. She had told the boy and his sister that they could go out into the garden, and said, "There are some flowers out there about which I am very careful. I do not want you to pick them."

So Johnny and Mary go out, and Johnny goes to work to do just what he was asked not to do. His sister says, "Johnny, did you not hear Mother tell us not to pick those flowers? Why pick them?"

"Because," says Johnny, "she loves me so, Mary. Don't you know how she loves me; how when I was sick, Mother gave up sleep and everything, and watched over me through the nights? Don't you know that she is sick there now because she loves me so? And so I am now going to do the very thing she told me not to do."

What would you think of a boy like that? And what do you think of the man or woman who make their boast of the love of God, and because God loves them, make God's love an excuse for rebellion against Him, and make God's love a reason for a worldly life?

Reuben Archer Torrey

. . .that you strive together with me in prayers to God for me. Romans 15:30 NKJV

T his evening I was walking in our little garden, meditating on the fact that Jesus Christ is the same yesterday, today, and forever. While meditating on His unchangeable love, power, and wisdom, I turned my meditation, as I went on, into prayer concerning myself. While applying likewise His unchangeable love, power, and wisdom both to my present spiritual and earthly circumstances—all at once the present need of the orphanage was brought to my mind. Immediately I was led to say to myself, *Jesus in His love and power has previously supplied me with what I have needed for the orphans. In the same unchangeable love and power, He will provide me with what I may need for the future.* A flow of joy came into my soul while realizing the unchangeableness of our adorable Lord.

George Müller

"Yet the LORD chose your ancestors as the objects of his love." Deuteronomy 10:15 NLT

*T*his is an ancient graveyard with the names Adam, Sheth, and Enosh. The names of past generations who were born and died, who loved and suffered, who stormed and fought through the world, are engraven on these solid slabs. But there is no inscription to record their worth or demerit. Just names and nothing more.

How strange to think that if Christ tarry, our names will be treated with the same apathy as these! But each person was the object of the love of God. Each was included in the redemptive purpose of our Lord. Each is living yet somewhere. Each will have to stand before the judgment bar of God. It is a stupendous thought to imagine the whole human race rooted in Adam like one vast far-spreading tree. Ah, reader, be sure that you art taken out of the first Adam and grafted into the second—the Lord Jesus.

F. B. Meyer

LOVE AND THE RAINBOW—JANUARY 18

Like the appearance of a rainbow in a cloud on a rainy day,
so was the appearance of the brightness all around it.
This was the appearance of the likeness of the glory of the LORD. Ezekiel 1:28 NKJV

*G*lory belongs to the Father and the Son: to the Father that He so loved the world that He gave His only begotten Son, to the Son that He so loved the world as to give up Himself. But there is equal glory due to the Holy Spirit, for He is that love of the Father and the Son to the world. Just so much as the first two persons of the Godhead glorify themselves by showing the astonishing greatness of their love and grace, just so much is that wonderful love and grace glorified by the Holy Spirit.

Christ purchased for us that we should have the favor of God and might enjoy His love, but this love is the Holy Spirit, which is but the indwelling of the Holy Spirit in the heart. Christ purchased for us spiritual joy and comfort, which is in a participation of God's joy and happiness, which joy and happiness is the Holy Spirit. The Holy Spirit is the sum of all good things.

Jonathan Edwards

January 19—Wonderful Love

"As the Father has loved me, so have I loved you.
Now remain in my love." John 15:9 NIV

*H*ave you ever noticed the difference between work and fruit? A machine can do work; only life can bear fruit. A law can compel work; only love can spontaneously bring forth fruit.

We are in danger of looking to Christ as a Savior and a supplier of every need, appointed by God, accepted and trusted by us, without any sense of the intensity of the personal affection in which Christ embraces us. He leads us to Himself to show us how identical His own life is with ours. Even as the Father loved Him, Jesus loves us. If we are to live like Him, as branches to be truly like the vine, we must share in this, too. Our life must have its breath and being in a heavenly love as much as His. What the Father's love was to Him, His love will be to us. If that love made Him the true vine, His love can make us true branches.

Andrew Murray

January 20—Walking in God's Love

And Enoch walked with God: and he was not; for God took him. Genesis 5:24 KJV

*W*alking with God implies our making progress or advances in the divine life. Walking, in the very first idea of the word, seems to suppose a progressive motion. A person who walks, though he moves slowly, yet he goes forward and does not continue in one place. So it is with those who walk with God.

Believers keep up and maintain their walk with God by reading of His holy Word. "Search the scriptures," says our blessed Lord, "for these are they that testify of Me." If we cease making the written Word of God our sole rule both as to faith and practice, we shall soon lie open to all manner of delusion and be in great danger of making a shipwreck of faith and a good conscience.

If you would walk with God, you will associate and keep company with those who do walk with Him. The primitive Christians, no doubt, kept up their vigor and first love by continuing in fellowship one with another.

George Whitefield

For men shall be. . .lovers of pleasures more than lovers of God. 2 Timothy 3:2, 4 KJV

Youth is the time when our passions are strongest—and, like unruly children, cry most loudly for indulgence. Youth is the time when we have generally our most health and strength. Death seems far away, and to enjoy ourselves in this life seems to be everything. Youth is the time when most people have few earthly cares or anxieties to take up their attention. And all these things help to make young people think of nothing except pleasure.

Time would not permit me to tell you all the fruits this love of pleasure produces, and all the ways in which it may harm you. All things that give a feeling of excitement for the time—all things that drown thought and keep the mind in a constant whirl, and all things that please the senses and delight the flesh—these are the sort of things that have mighty power at your time of life. They owe their power to the love of pleasure. There is no surer way to get a seared conscience and a hard heart toward the things of God than to give way to the desires of the flesh and mind.

J. C. Ryle

RAINBOW OF LOVE—JANUARY 22

Love is patient, love is kind. It does not envy, it does not boast, it is not proud. Love does not delight in evil but rejoices with the truth. 1 Corinthians 13:4, 6 NIV

Love is like light. You have seen a scientist take a beam of light and pass it through a prism. You have seen it come out on the other side of the prism broken up into its component colors—red, orange, yellow, green, blue, violet, and all the colors of the rainbow. In the same way, Paul passes this thing, love, through the magnificent prism of his inspired intellect. It comes out on the other side broken up into its elements. And in these few words we have what one might call the spectrum of love, the analysis of love.

The spectrum of love has nine ingredients: patience, kindness, generosity, humility, courtesy, unselfishness, good temper, guilelessness, and sincerity. These make up the supreme gift, the stature of the perfect Christian. You will observe that all are in relation to men, in relation to life, in relation to the known today and the near tomorrow, and not to the unknown eternity.

Henry Drummond

JANUARY 23—LED BY LOVE

Keep yourselves in the love of God; look forward to the mercy of our LORD Jesus Christ that leads to eternal life. Jude 21 NRSV

I found that there were two thirsts in me—the one after the creature comforts and the other after the Lord, the Creator, and His Son Jesus Christ. I saw that all the world could do me no good. If I had had a king's diet, palace, and attendance, all would have been as nothing because nothing gave me comfort but the Lord by His power. I saw the great love of God and was filled with admiration at the infiniteness of it.

One day, when I had been walking alone and came home, I was taken up in the love of God. I could not but admire the greatness of His love. While I was in that condition, I clearly saw that all these troubles were good for me for the trial of my faith. I saw all through these troubles and temptations that my living faith was raised.

George Fox

JANUARY 24—THE LORD IS GOOD

Now that you have tasted that the LORD is good. . . 1 Peter 2:3 NIV

I shall never forget the hour when I first discovered that God was really good. It had never dawned on me that it meant He was actually and practically good, with the same kind of goodness He has commanded us to have. The expression "the goodness of God" had seemed to me nothing more than a sort of heavenly statement, which I could not be expected to understand. Then one day in my reading of the Bible I came across the words "O taste and see that the Lord is good," and suddenly they meant something. What does it mean to be good?

I can never express what this meant to me. I had such a view of the actual goodness of God that I saw nothing could possibly go wrong under His care, and it seemed to me that no one could ever be anxious again. Over and over again I have been brought up short by the words "the Lord is good." I have seen that it was simply unthinkable that a God who was good could have done the bad things I had imagined.

Hannah Whitall Smith

And we know that all things work together for good to them that love God,
to them who are the called according to his purpose. Romans 8:28 KJV

*T*here are two things that I have always looked upon as difficult. The one is to make the wicked sad, and the other is to make the godly joyful. To cure both these troubles, I would prescribe them to take, now and then, a little of this cordial, this comfort for the heart: "All things work together for good to them that love God."

It is not a matter wavering or doubtful. The apostle does not say, "We hope." A Christian may come not merely to a vague opinion, but to a certainty of what he holds. Though a Christian has not a perfect knowledge of the mysteries of the gospel, yet he has a certain knowledge. The Spirit of God imprints heavenly truths upon the heart as with the point of a diamond.

Thomas Watson

Love and the Cannibals—January 26

"Because he loves me," says the LORD, "I will rescue him;
I will protect him, for he acknowledges my name." Psalm 91:14 NIV

*O*ne day, while working as a missionary on the Pacific Island of Tanna, I heard an unusual bleating among my few remaining goats, as if they were being killed. I rushed to the goat house and found myself instantly surrounded by a band of armed men. Their weapons were raised, and I expected the next moment to die. I assured them I was not afraid to die, for at death my Savior would take me to heaven and that I would be far happier than on earth. My only desire to live was to make them happy by teaching them to love Jesus Christ my Lord.

I then lifted up my hands and eyes to the heavens and prayed aloud for Jesus to bless all the Tannese and to protect me or take me to heaven as He saw to be for the best. One after another, they slipped away from me, and Jesus restrained them again. Did ever a mother run more quickly to protect her crying child in danger's hour than the Lord Jesus hastens to answer believing prayer and send help to His servants?

John G. Paton

*"You shall not covet your neighbor's house. You shall not covet your neighbor's wife,
or his manservant or maidservant, his ox or donkey, or anything
that belongs to your neighbor." Exodus 20:17 NIV*

*T*he Bible says that the love of money is a root of all kinds of evil. The tenth commandment against coveting has therefore been properly called a "root extractor," because it would tear up and destroy this root. Matthew tells us that the deceitfulness of riches chokes the Word of God. Isn't that true of many businesspeople today? They are so engrossed with their affairs that they have no time for religion. They lose sight of their souls and their eternal welfare in their desire to amass wealth. They do not even hesitate to sell their souls to the devil. People say, "We must make money, and if God's law stands in the way, brush it aside."

Recall how Judas's love of money lured him into the betrayal of his divine friend into the hand of His murderers. You ask me how you are to cast this unclean spirit out of your heart. Make up your mind that by the grace of God you will overcome the spirit of selfishness. You must overcome it, or it will overcome you.

Dwight Lyman Moody

JANUARY 28—LOVE AND STEADFAST FAITH

*But let all who take refuge in you be glad; let them ever sing for joy. Spread your
protection over them, that those who love your name may rejoice in you. Psalm 5:11 NIV*

A man who has lost his right eye is unable to defend himself in battle because his shield hides his left eye, and so he has no sight to defend himself from the enemy. In the same way, he who has lost the right eye of true faith is unable to withstand or fight against his spiritual enemy, the devil.

We must trust steadfastly that nothing may harm us any more than God will allow it, and all things that He sends come for the best. And let no wealth of this failing world, neither tribulation, draw our hearts from firm belief in God. Let us not put our belief or trust in charms or in dreams or any other fantasies, but only in Almighty God.

To believe in God, as St. Augustine says, is in belief to cling to God through love, and to seek actively to fulfill His will. For no man truly believes in God except he who loves God.

John Wycliffe

But I am like an olive tree flourishing in the house of God;
I trust in God's unfailing love for ever and ever. Psalm 52:8 NIV

*T*rust sees God doing things here and now. Yes, and more. It rises to a lofty eminence and, looking into the invisible and the eternal, realizes that God has done things and regards them as being already done. Trust brings eternity into the annals and happenings of time, transmutes the substance of hope into the reality of fulfillment, and changes promise into present possession. We know when we trust just as we know when we see, just as we are conscious of our sense of touch. Trust sees, receives, and holds. Trust is its own witness.

Yet, quite often, faith is too weak to obtain God's greatest good immediately. It has to wait in loving, strong, prayerful, and pressing obedience until it grows in strength and is able to bring down the eternal into the realms of experience and time. Trust, in a historical fact or in a mere record, may be a very passive thing, but trust in a person vitalizes the quality, makes it productive, and makes it known with love.

Edward McKendree Bounds

YIELD TO LOVE—JANUARY 30

Surely it was for my benefit that I suffered such anguish. In your love you kept me from
the pit of destruction; you have put all my sins behind your back. Isaiah 38:17 NIV

*L*et us keep in mind that we cannot taste the love of God in our afflictions unless we are persuaded that they are rods with which our Father chastises us for our sins. Although God's hand falls upon those in His house and those outside, it falls upon the former to show His special care for them. The true solution of our problem is as follows: Anyone who knows and is persuaded that God reprimands him must promptly go on to consider that God afflicts him because He loves him. For if God did not love him, He would not care about his salvation. God offers Himself as a father to all those who endure correction. In short then, when God corrects us, He does so only as our Father, provided we yield and obey.

John Calvin

January 31—The Meaning of "Love Your Neighbor"

The commandments, "Do not commit adultery," "Do not murder," "Do not steal," "Do not covet," and whatever other commandment there may be, are summed up in this one rule: "Love your neighbor as yourself." Romans 13:9 NIV

A man ought to love his neighbor equally and fully as well as himself because his neighbor is equally created of God and is fully redeemed by the blood of our Savior Jesus Christ. Out of which commandment of love spring these: Kill not your neighbor; defile not his wife; bear no false witness against him. You must not only avoid doing these things in deed, but you must also not covet in your heart his house, his wife, his manservant, maidservant, ox, donkey, or whatsoever is his. These laws, pertaining unto our neighbor, are not fulfilled in the sight of God except with love.

For he who has trust in anyone, whether in heaven or in earth, save in God and His Son Jesus, can see no cause to love God with all his heart. And likewise, against this law, "Love your neighbor as yourself," I may obey no worldly power to do anything to hurt my neighbor even if he is an unbeliever.

William Tyndale

February 1—The Sword of Love

Disregarding another person's faults preserves love; telling about them separates close friends. Proverbs 17:9 NLT

*C*an a person hate the world enough to change it, and yet love it enough to think it worth changing? Can he look up at its colossal evil without feeling despair? I want to love my neighbor not because he is I, but precisely because he is not I. I want to adore the world, not as a person likes looking at his image in a mirror because it is one's self, but as one loves a woman because she is entirely different. If souls are separate, love is possible. A man may be said loosely to love himself, but he can hardly fall in love with himself.

Christianity is a sword that separates and sets free. No other philosophy makes God actually rejoice in the separation of the universe into living souls. But according to Christianity, this separation between God and man is sacred, because it is eternal. For a person to love God, it is necessary that there should be not only a God to be loved, but a person to love Him.

Gilbert K. Chesterton

I revere your commandments, which I love, and I will
meditate on your statutes. Psalm 119:48 NRSV

The first requirement of real life is something to love, and the second requirement is something to revere. Each of the elements is essential. Each deprived of the other is robbed of its dynamic. Neither can lift if the other be absent. Love without reverence becomes a purely carnal sentiment and resides in the channels of the flesh. Reverence without love is like cold moonlight and will never enrich the heart with the presence of gracious flowers. Love without reverence is a destructive fever; reverence without love is a perpetual frost. True love kneels in reverence; true reverence yearns in love.

I sometimes take down from my bookshelves a little book of devotions and read one of its quaint and engaging titles: "Calvary is the true academy of love." If I want a school where love is taught and revealed, I must seek the academy of Calvary! The teaching is superlatively impressive, and even the dullest scholar makes progress in the school. We are to go into the academy of Calvary, which is the all-excelling school of love.

John Henry Jowett

BOBBY THE MISSIONARY—FEBRUARY 3

"'From the lips of children and infants you have ordained praise'?" Matthew 21:16 NIV

We have a little abandoned boy of six years old in our hospital. He was brought in cursing and swearing. He had never heard a good word in all his life. He had an abscess in his back. That was about a year ago, and he can only just now stand.

The head nurse of the ward did not scold or preach to Bobby. By degrees, she taught him little prayers. And now if she is busy, he calls, "Sister, Sister, I have not said my prayers." It is a real speaking to God with him. The new patients stop and listen to hear him.

It is as Christ meant when He said that the little child might be the best preacher of us all. So he is a little missionary and quite an influence among the rough men patients, and they take care of him. Never a word is spoken now to him that a little child ought not to hear. One of the poor men who had to be taken into a medical ward sent a message to Bobby from his deathbed. Bobby has the real thing in his heart, the true religion.

Florence Nightingale

February 4—Grounded in Love

...but to your name give glory, for the sake of your steadfast love and your faithfulness.
Psalm 115:1 NRSV

Why should anything have my heart but Christ? He loves me; He loves me with love that goes beyond knowledge. He loves me, and He shall have me. He loves me, and I will love Him. His love stripped Him of all for my sake. *Lord, let my love strip me of all for Your sake.* I am a son of love, an object of love, a monument of love, of love freely given, of distinguishing love, of special love, and of love that passes knowledge. I walk in love—in love to God, in love to men, in holy love, and in genuine love.

If you would improve this love, keep yourself in it. He who would live a sweet, comfortable, joyful life must live a very holy life. To this end, you must take root and be grounded in love; that is, you must be well settled and established in this love, if indeed you would improve it.

John Bunyan

February 5—Love and Prayers

"But I tell you: Love your enemies and
pray for those who persecute you." Matthew 5:44 NIV

We are all selfish by nature, and our selfishness is very apt to stick to us even when we are converted. There is a tendency in us to think only of our own souls, our own spiritual conflicts, our own progress in religion, and to forget others. Against this tendency, we all have need to watch and strive, and not the least in our prayers. We should try to bear in our hearts the whole world, the unbelievers, the body of true believers, the churches, the country in which we live, the congregation to which we belong, the homes in which we visit, the friends, and the relations we are connected with. For each and all of these, we should plead. This is the highest love. They love me best who love me in their prayers.

J. C. Ryle

Hold fast the form of sound words, which thou hast heard of me,
in faith and love which is in Christ Jesus. 2 Timothy 1:13 KJV

Sojourner Truth's mother talked to her of God. From these conversations, her mind drew the conclusion that God was a great man and, being located high in the sky, could see all that transpired on the earth. She believed He not only saw but also noted down all her actions in a great book.

At first she heard Jesus mentioned in reading or speaking, but had received from what she heard no impression that He was any other than an eminent man, like a Washington or a Lafayette. Now He appeared to her so mild, so good, and so every way lovely, and He loved her so much! And how strange that He had always loved her and she had never known it! And how great a blessing He conferred, in that He should stand between her and God! And God was no longer a terror and a dread to her.

In the light of her great happiness, the world was clad in new beauty, the very air sparkled as with diamonds and was redolent of heaven.

Sojourner Truth

IMAGE OF CHRIST—FEBRUARY 7

. . .make my joy complete by being like-minded, having the same love,
being one in spirit and purpose. Philippians 2:1–2 NIV

When Christians have sunk down into a low state, they neither have nor can have the same love and confidence toward each other as when they are all alive and active and living holy lives. If Christian love is the love of the image of Christ in His people, then it can be exercised only where that image really exists. Merely knowing that they belong to the church, or seeing them occasionally at the Communion table, will not produce Christian love unless they see the image of Christ.

So if a member of the church finds his brethren cold toward him, there is but one way to restore it. It is by being revived himself, and pouring out from his eyes and from his life the splendor of the image of Christ. This spirit will catch and spread in the church, confidence will be renewed, and brotherly love prevail again.

Charles Finney

February 8—The Best of the Three

And now faith, hope, and love abide, these three;
and the greatest of these is love. 1 Corinthians 13:13 NRSV

*T*he apostle says love is greater than the other two—that is, faith and
hope—for the more richly love dwells in a man, the better the man in
whom it dwells. For when we ask whether someone is a good man, we
are not asking what he believes or hopes, but what he loves. He who loves
rightly believes and hopes rightly. Likewise, he who does not love believes
in vain, even if what he believes is true. An example of this would be if a
man hopes for life eternal—and who is there who does not love that?—
and yet does not love righteousness without which no one comes to life
eternal.

The true faith of Christ is faith that works through love. And what
faith yet lacks in love, it asks that it may receive, it seeks that it may find,
and knocks that it may be opened unto it. For faith achieves what the law
commands.

Augustine

February 9—Love and the Saint's Rest

Put me on trial, LORD, and cross-examine me. Test my motives and affections.
For I am constantly aware of your unfailing love, and I have lived according to your truth.
Psalm 26:2–3 NLT

*C*hristian, believe this and think on it: You shall be eternally embraced
in the arms of that love which was from everlasting and will extend to
everlasting. You will be embraced by that love which brought the Son of
God's love from heaven to earth, from earth to the cross, from the cross
to the grave, from the grave to glory. You will be in the arms of that love
which was weary, hungry, tempted, scorned, scourged, buffeted, spit upon,
crucified, and pierced; which did fast, pray, teach, heal, weep, sweat, bleed,
and die. It will be loving and rejoicing, not loving and sorrowing. Yes, it
will make Satan's court ring with the news that the saints are arrived safe
at the bosom of Christ, out of the reach of hell forever.

Richard Baxter

For I am persuaded that neither. . .height nor depth, nor any other created thing,
shall be able to separate us from the love of God which is in Christ Jesus our LORD.
Romans 8:38–39 NKJV

The nature of God, as testified by John, is love. Nothing but love can bind the universe together; therefore, God, the life, the spring of all, must be love. Wrath, the opposite of love, is that which disunites; therefore, it cannot really exist in God. There can be nothing in God contrary to love; else, He would be divided. If God's nature is love, then He must be just, faithful, true, merciful, and so on.

Adam and Eve enjoyed the unceasing streams of love. But sin filled them with fear, torment, condemnation, and wrath. These would have eternally kept them for receiving any influence of eternal love. But Jesus came to destroy the works of the devil, and to prepare our hearts for receiving again the happiness and comfort of God's eternal love.

Barton W. Stone

OBEDIENT LOVE—FEBRUARY 11

"Choose to love the LORD your God and to obey him
and commit yourself to him, for he is your life."
Deuteronomy 30:20 NLT

It is a very great thing to obey, to live under a superior and not to be one's own master, for it is much safer to be subject than it is to command. Many live in obedience more from necessity than from love. Such become discontented and dejected on the slightest pretext. They will never gain peace of mind unless they subject themselves wholeheartedly for the love of God.

Do not trust too much in your own opinions, but be willing to listen to those of others. If, though your own be good, you accept another's opinion for love of God, you will gain much more merit; for I have often heard that it is safer to listen to advice and take it than to give it. It may happen, too, that while one's own opinion may be good, refusal to agree with others when reason and occasion demand it is a sign of pride and obstinacy.

Thomas à Kempis

FEBRUARY 12—SURRENDERED LOVE

...stand firm in the LORD in this way, my beloved. Philippians 4:1 NRSV

Could there be a sadder proof of the extent and reality of the Fall than the deep-seated distrust of our loving Lord and Master, which makes us hesitate to give ourselves entirely up to Him. The real secret of an unsatisfied life lies too often in an unsurrendered will. And yet how foolish this is!

Do we fancy that we are wiser than He, that our love for ourselves is more tender and strong than His, or that we know ourselves better than He does? What would be the feelings of an earthly bridegroom if he discovered that his bride-elect were dreading to marry him, for fear that when he had the power, he should render her life insupportable? Yet how many of the Lord's redeemed ones treat Him just so! No wonder they are neither happy nor satisfied!

Hudson Taylor

FEBRUARY 13—FORTRESS OF LOVE

Keep me as the apple of the eye,
hide me under the shadow of thy wings. Psalm 17:8 KJV

Our ignorance of God gives us all sorts of wrong ideas about Him. We think He is an angry judge who is on the watch for our slightest faults, or a harsh taskmaster determined to exact from us the uttermost service, or a self-absorbed deity demanding His full measure of honor and glory, or a far-off sovereign concerned only with His own affairs and indifferent to our welfare.

But I can assert boldly and without fear of contradiction that it is impossible for anyone who really knows God to have such uncomfortable thoughts about Him. Plenty of outward discomforts there may be and many earthly sorrows and trials, but through them all, the soul that knows God cannot but dwell inwardly in a fortress of perfect peace. If we would really listen unto God, which means not only hearing Him but believing what we hear, we could not fail to know that, just because He is God, He cannot do other than care for us as He cares for the apple of His eye.

Hannah Whitall Smith

*"If you want to be my follower you must love me
more than your own father and mother." Luke 14:26 NLT*

*I*n Jacksonville at the house in which I stayed, my attention was attracted by a little boy, who bore a different name from the household. Some years before, his father and mother had come home with their five children to have them educated. It was arranged that the children should be received into various families—treated as part of them—and that the father and mother should return to India. The mother came to this friend's home and stayed a few days along with the boy. The night before she had to leave, sitting with the lady of the house, she told her how she wished to leave him without a tear at parting. The struggle this would cost, the lady well knew.

The next morning the lady overheard a sobbing prayer for strength. In a short time, the mother came down with a smiling, cheerful face; and looking so, she took leave of her boy. She went with her husband to India. A short year later, she met her Savior. And would not a welcome await her there, who had so loved Him here and so cheerfully served Him?

Dwight Lyman Moody

TRIUMPHANT LOVE—FEBRUARY 15

*My God in his steadfast love will meet me; my God will let me
look in triumph on my enemies. Psalm 59:10 NRSV*

*W*ould you know the blessing of all blessings? It is this God of love dwelling in your soul and killing every root of bitterness that is the pain and torment of every earthly, selfish love. For all wants are satisfied, all disorders of nature are removed, no life is any longer a burden, every day is a day of peace. Everything you meet becomes a help to you because everything you see or do is all done in the sweet, gentle element of love. For as love has no selfish purposes, wills nothing but its own increase, so everything is as oil to its flame. The spirit of love does not want to be rewarded, honored, or esteemed. Its only desire is to propagate itself and become the blessing and happiness of everyone who wants it.

William Law

February 16—The Bridegroom's Friends

In love of the brethren be tenderly affectionate one to another;
in honor preferring one another. Romans 12:10 ASV

If we are married to Jesus Christ, we shall not only reverence the bridegroom, but we shall also love and honor the bridegroom's friends. Jesus says, "By this, shall all men know that you are My disciples, if you love one another."

"By this we know," says the beloved disciple, "that we have passed from death to life because we love the brethren." Observe love for the brethren without limit of whatever denomination. This was the case of the primitive Christians. They were all of one heart and of one mind. It was said of them (Oh, that it could be said of us!): "See how these Christians love one another!"

Persons who are married take one another for better or for worse, for richer or for poorer, to love and to cherish each other in sickness and in health. And if we are married to Jesus Christ, we shall be willing to bear His cross as well as to wear His crown. They will cry out, "Crown Him, crown Him," when others are crying out, "Crucify Him, crucify Him."

George Whitefield

February 17—The Call of Love

"But the hour is coming, and now is, when the true worshipers will
worship the Father in spirit and truth." John 4:23 NKJV

Faith is spiritual, and God who is a spirit delights in it for that reason. Years of prayer saying, church going, or ceremonies may only be displeasing in the sight of Jehovah if done with self-righteous pride. But a glance from the eye of true faith is spiritual, and it is therefore dear to Him.

Your own heart will not prosper unless it is filled with intense concern to bless your fellow men. The life of your soul lies in faith. Its health lies in love. He who does not long to lead others to Jesus has never been under the spell of love himself. Get to the work of the Lord—the work of love. Begin at home. Next, visit your neighbors. Then, enlighten the village or the street in which you live.

Charles Haddon Spurgeon

I love those who love me, and those who seek me diligently find me. Proverbs 8:17 NRSV

You may overlove the things of the earth. You may love wine too much and silver too much, but you cannot love God too much. If it were possible to exceed, excess here would be a virtue, but it is because of our sin that we cannot love God enough. So it may be said, "How weak is our love to God!" If we could love God far more than we do, yet it would not be proportional to His worth. There is no danger of excess in our love to God.

You may love worldly things, and they die and leave you. Riches take wings. Relations drop away. There is nothing here abiding. But if you love God, He is called a sun for comfort, a rock for eternity. He abides forever. We see it is better to love God than the world.

Thomas Watson

ACTIVE LOVE—FEBRUARY 19

Be kind and compassionate to one another,
forgiving each other, just as in Christ God forgave you.
Ephesians 4:32 NIV

Love is active. Have you ever noticed how much of Christ's life was spent in doing kind things? Run over it with that in view, and you will find that He spent a great proportion of His time simply in making people happy—in doing good turns to people. What God has put in our power is the happiness of those about us, and that is largely to be secured by our being kind to them.

"The greatest thing," says someone, "a man can do for his heavenly Father is to be kind to some of His other children." I wonder why it is that we are not all kinder than we are. The world needs it. How easily it is done. How instantaneously it acts. How infallibly it is remembered. How superabundantly it pays itself back—for there is no debtor in the world so honorable, so superbly honorable, as love. Love is success, love is happiness, love is life.

Henry Drummond

*"Let the little children come to me, and do not hinder them, for the
kingdom of God belongs to such as these." Mark 10:14 NIV*

*O*ur children must not only find in Jesus their Savior; they must find in
Him their hero, too. Say to yourself, "I will so present my Master as a hero
as to attract the adoring homage of my children." Would you be without
any heroic subject matter? Your eyes are closed and sealed if you do not
see the heroic glowing upon every page of the sacred story! His splendid
bravery; His tremendous hatred of all meanness and sin; His solitude in
the night; His refusal of a popular crown, when the sovereignty would
mean compromise with the powers of darkness! Let these be unfolded
with the same effort and vivid realization which we make when we seek to
unveil the heroism of earthly achievers, and our boys and girls will go on
their knees before the unveiling with reverent admiration and homage.

The Lord will become the children's staff of life. Their worship will
become their desire. Their loving will become their longing. Their admiration will become aspiration. Their faith will become their hope.

John Henry Jowett

FEBRUARY 21—UNFOLDING LOVE

*. . .and to goodness, knowledge, and to knowledge, self-control; and to self-control,
perseverance; and to perseverance, godliness; and to godliness,
brotherly kindness; and to brotherly kindness, love. 2 Peter 1:5–7 NIV*

*S*o long as sin is in the world, love must make war against it. The
first step of love is the offer of pardon through the atoning blood of
Jesus Christ. But a pardoned criminal is not necessarily a good citizen.
Pardon has changed his relation to the law but not his hostility toward the
governor. A change must take place within him.

The second step in the conquest of the soul by love divine is regen-
eration, or the New Birth. It is a change wrought within the soul by the
power of the Holy Spirit, creating within the soul a new spiritual life, a life
of loyalty and love. It implies future germination, growth, and bearing of
fruit. It is to spread its branches until it fills the heart, and by absorbing all
the fertility of the soil and by completely overshadowing all other plants,
destroys their life. The positive work of spiritual adornment, strength, and
growth must go on so long as the soul is capable of advancement.

Daniel Steele

This is how we know who. . .the children of the devil are: Anyone who does not do
what is right is not a child of God; nor is anyone who does not love his brother.
1 John 3:10 NIV

I formed a close friendship with a brother who was also a divinity student. Because we loved one another so much and were so happy in one another's company, we thought to rent lodging to share, and that in this way we might mutually help one another.

Unfortunately, we were not aware that because God is greatly glorified by the love and union of His people, Satan particularly hates it and will, therefore, in every possible way seek to divide them. We ought to have especially prayed that the Lord would keep us together in brotherly love. Instead, I do not think that we at all feared disunion, as we loved one another so much. Our great adversary soon got an advantage by our neglecting prayer concerning this point, and we were disunited. Unity was not fully restored between us until after we had been for some time separated.

George Müller

STAND ON LOVE—FEBRUARY 23

Don't just pretend that you love others. Really love them. Hate what
is wrong. Stand on the side of the good. Romans 12:9 NLT

T he prophet Nehemiah had a perfect right to take tax money from the people, but he did not. Not a word could be said even by his critics, if he did. He was doing a priceless work and might justly claim his support. On the other hand, the people were very poor, and he would have a larger influence over them if he were prepared to stand on their level and to share with them.

Often we must forego our evident rights and liberties in order to influence others for Christ. Do not always stand on your rights. Instead, live for others, making any sacrifice in order to save some—even as Christ loved us and gave Himself for us.

All around you, people are doing things that they say are perfectly legitimate. They call you narrow-minded and bigoted because you do not join with them. They are always arguing with you in an effort to prove you are wrong. But your supreme law is your attitude to your Master: "I cannot do otherwise for the love of Jesus."

F. B. Meyer

FEBRUARY 24—TRUE CHRISTIAN LOVE

And watch as I take those who call themselves true believers but are nothing of the kind, . . . as I strip off their pretensions and they're forced to acknowledge it's you that I've loved. Revelation 3:9 TM

I held my Sabbath school at the house of a free colored man, whose name I deem it imprudent to mention. I had at one time over forty scholars, and those of the right sort, ardently desiring to learn. We loved each other, and to leave them at the close of the Sabbath was a severe cross indeed.

They not only possessed loving hearts but also brave ones. I loved them with a love stronger than anything I have experienced since. It is sometimes said that we slaves do not love and confide in each other. In answer to this assertion, I can say I never loved any or confided in any people more than my fellow-slaves. I believe we would have died for each other.

What I have said respecting and against religion, I mean strictly to apply to the slaveholding religion of this land and with no possible reference to Christianity proper. I love the pure, peaceable, and impartial Christianity of Christ.

Frederick Douglass

FEBRUARY 25—RECEIVE AND GIVE LOVE

"I have obeyed my Father's commands and remain in his love." John 15:10 NIV

*J*esus has said that by obedience we live in His love. He tells that this was the way He lived in the Father's love. As the vine, so is the branch. His life, strength, and joy had been in the love of the Father.

He was made like us in all things, that we might be like Him in all things. He opened up a path in which we may walk even as He walked. He took our human nature to teach us how to wear it. He showed us how obedience is the only way to live in the favor of God and enter into His glory. And now He comes to instruct and encourage us, and asks us to keep His commandments, even as He kept His Father's commandments and lived in His love.

Dear Lord, I am only beginning to comprehend how exactly the life of the vine is to be that of the branch, too. You are the vine, because the Father loved You and poured His love through You. My life as a branch is to be like You, a receiving and a giving out of heavenly love.

Andrew Murray

May those who love your salvation always say, "The LORD be exalted!" Psalm 40:16 NIV

Will you say that you are afraid to come to God? Your fear is needless. You shall not be cast out, if you will but come in the way of faith in Christ. Our God is not an austere man. Our Father in heaven is full of mercy, love, and grace. I yield to none in desire to promote the love, mercy, and tenderness of God the Father.

We know that God is holy. We know He is just. We believe that He can be angry with them who go on still in sin. But we also believe that to those who draw near to Him in Christ Jesus, He is most merciful, most loving, most tender, and most compassionate. We tell you that the cross of Jesus Christ was the result and consequence of that love.

Draw near in faith by that living way, Christ Jesus to the Father. As the father did to the prodigal son when he ran to meet him—fell on his neck and kissed him—so will God the Father do to that soul who draws near to Him in the name of Christ.

J. C. Ryle

Love and Sacrifice—February 27

If I. . .surrender my body to the flames, but have not love,
I gain nothing. 1 Corinthians 13:3 NIV

Love is the universal language. It will take you years to speak in Chinese or in the dialects of India. From the day you land in a foreign country, that language of love, understood by all, will be pouring forth its unconscious eloquence. It is not your words but your character that is the message.

In the heart of Africa, I have come across men and women who remembered the only white man they ever saw before—David Livingstone. As you cross his footsteps in that continent, men's faces light up as they speak of the kind doctor who passed there years ago. They could not understand him, but they felt the love that beat in his heart. Take into your new sphere of labor that simple charm, and your lifework must succeed. You can take nothing greater; you need take nothing less. You may take every accomplishment, you may be braced for every sacrifice, but if you have not love, it will profit you and the cause of Christ nothing.

Henry Drummond

. . .and I will dwell in the house of the LORD forever. Psalm 23:6 NIV

*G*reat pains had been taken by my parents to instill the doctrines of Christianity into my mind, and I had no difficulty in understanding the theory of our free salvation by the atonement of our Savior. I really began to feel the necessity and value of a personal application of the provisions of that atonement to my own case.

The change was like what may be supposed would take place were it possible to cure a case of "color blindness." A sense of deep obligation to Him for His mercy has influenced my conduct ever since. But I shall not again refer to the inner spiritual life, which I believe then began, nor do I intend to specify with any prominence the evangelistic labors to which the love of Christ has since impelled me. I will speak, not so much of what has been done, as of what still remains to be performed, before the gospel can be said to be preached to all nations.

In the glow of love, which Christianity inspires, I soon resolved to devote my life to the alleviation of human misery. Turning this idea over in my mind, I therefore set myself to obtain a medical education, in order to be qualified for that enterprise.

David Livingstone

MARCH 1—LOVE WITHOUT DOUBT

For the one who doubts is like a wave of the sea, driven and tossed by the wind. James 1:6 NRSV

I knew one devoted Christian whose religious life was one long torment of doubt. He thought that perfect confidence could only arise from a feeling that he was good enough to be worthy of God's love, but he felt this would be presumptive. But our confidence does not come from our own goodness but from the goodness of God. While we never can be and never ought to be satisfied with goodness in ourselves, there cannot possibly be any question to one who believes the Bible as to the all-sufficiency of God's goodness.

If you believe one day that God loves you and is favorable to you and the next day doubt His love, and fear that He is angry with you, does it not stand to reason that you must waver in your experience from joy to misery? Only a steadfast faith in His love and care could give you an unwavering experience.

Hannah Whitall Smith

May the LORD direct your hearts to the love of God and to the steadfastness of Christ.
2 Thessalonians 3:5 NRSV

We cannot love that which we do not know. That our love may be drawn forth to God, we must know that He has a fullness of grace to cleanse us and a fullness of glory to crown us. He has a fullness not only of sufficiency but also of redundancy. He is a sea of goodness without bottom and banks. God has an innate propensity to dispense mercy and grace. He drops them as honey from the honeycomb.

We set a high value upon God as being the most sublime and infinite good. The stars vanish when the sun appears. All other things vanish in our thoughts when the sun of righteousness shines in His full splendor. The soul who loves God rejoices in Him as in his treasure and rests in Him as in his center. The heart is so set upon God that it desires no more. We desire that His interest may prevail. Our prayer is that His name may be held in honor and that His gospel, which is the rod of His strength, may, like Aaron's rod, blossom and bring forth fruit.

Thomas Watson

INSEPARABLE LOVE—MARCH 3

If one were to give all the wealth of his house for love,
it would be utterly scorned. Song of Songs 8:7 NIV

Love is inseparable when a man's mind is inflamed with great love and clings to Christ by inseparable thought. Such a man does not allow Christ to be any moment out of his mind. As though he were bound in the heart, he thinks upon and draws his spirit from God. Therefore, the love of Christ so grows in the heart of the lover of God and despiser of the world that it may not be overcome by any other affection or love. When a man clings to Christ continuously, thinking upon Him, forgetting Him for no other occasion, then man's love is said to be inseparable and everlasting.

John Wycliffe

March 4—Love's Counterfeit

...pursue righteousness, faith, love and peace. 2 Timothy 2:22 NIV

There is nothing more beautiful on earth than a pure love, and there is nothing so blighting as lust. I do not know of a quicker, shorter way down to hell than by adultery and the kindred sins. The Bible says that with the heart man believeth unto righteousness, but lust will drive all natural affection out of a man's heart.

May God show us what a fearful sin it is! The idea of making light of it! I do not know of any sin that will make a man run down to ruin more quickly. I am appalled when I think of what is going on in the world, of so many young men living impure lives and talking about the virtue of women as if it didn't amount to anything. This sin is coming in upon us like a dark shroud at the present day.

Dwight Lyman Moody

March 5—Love and Language

Out of the same mouth proceedeth blessing and cursing...these things ought not so to be. James 3:10 KJV

People often ask, "How can I keep from swearing?" I will tell you. If God puts His love into your heart, you will have no desire to curse Him. I was preaching one day in the open air, when a man drove up in a fine carriage, and after listening a little while, he put the whip to his fine-looking steed, and away he went.

Later, I visited him at his home. "I am told that God has blessed you above all men in this part of the country. He has given you wealth, a beautiful Christian wife, and seven lovely children. I do not know if it is true, but I hear that all He gets in return is cursing and blasphemy."

The man said, "What you say is true. But you don't know anything about a businessman's troubles. When he is harassed and tormented the whole time, he can't help swearing."

"Yes," I said, "he can. I used to swear myself." I began to tell him about Christ in the heart and how that would take the temptation to swear out of a man. At the next church prayer meeting, the man was there. He said, "My friends, I want to have you pray for my salvation."

Thirty-odd years later I spoke to the man. He said, "I have never had a desire to swear since then. It was all taken away."

Dwight Lyman Moody

I prayed to the LORD my God and confessed: "O LORD, the great and awesome God,
who keeps his covenant of love with all who love him and obey his commands."
Daniel 9:4 NIV

Obedience is love fulfilling every command, and love expressing itself. Obedience, therefore, is not a hard demand made upon us. Love delights to obey and please whom it loves. There are no hardships in love. There are no impossible tasks for love. Obedience runs ahead of all and every command. It is love obeying by anticipation. They greatly err, and even sin, who declare that people are bound to commit iniquity, either because of environment or heredity or tendency. God's commands are ways of pleasantness, and their paths peace.

Loving obedience puts us where we can ask anything in God's name with the assurance that He will do it. Loving obedience brings us into the prayer realm and makes us beneficiaries of the wealth of Christ and of the riches of His grace. Cheerful obedience to God qualifies us to pray effectually. This obedience must be loving, constant, always doing the Father's will, and cheerfully following the path of God's commands.

Edward McKendree Bounds

LOVE'S FOUNDATION—MARCH 7

Righteousness and justice are the foundation of your throne; steadfast
love and faithfulness go before you. Psalm 89:14 NRSV

Our minds cannot come to rest in tranquility unless they arrive at the free love of God. Since we are not to seek the base of our salvation anywhere but in Christ, we must try to find out where He came to us from and why He was offered up to be our Savior. Scripture distinctly teaches both truths: Faith in Christ means life to all people, and Christ had this life because God loved mankind and would not let us perish.

Christ means to do nothing else than establish the love of God as the foundation of our salvation. When we try to go beyond this, the Spirit Himself slams the door in our face. God's love is founded in His own will and purpose. Christ does not declare that He was led to deliver us because He found us worthy of such a blessing. On the contrary, He attributes the glory of our deliverance solely to His love. Faith looks to Christ rightly when it sees in Him the heart of God overflowing with love.

John Calvin

MARCH 8—LOVE AND THE FIRST COMMANDMENT

You shall love the LORD your God with all your heart, and with all
your soul, and with all your might. Deuteronomy 6:5 NRSV

*I*t is not possible to sin any sin at all, except a person break the first commandment beforehand. Now the first commandment is divided into two verses: "Your Lord God is one God; and you shall love your Lord God with all your heart, with all your soul, with all your power, and with all your might." The whole cause why I sin against any secondary decree is that this love is not in my heart. If this love were written in my heart and were it full and perfect in my soul, it would keep my heart from consenting unto any sin.

If my heart believed and felt the infinite benefits and kindness of God toward me, and understood and earnestly believed the many covenants of mercy wherewith God has bound Himself to be mine wholly with all His power, love, mercy, and might, then should I love Him with all my heart, soul, power, and might. Because of that love I should always keep His commandments.

William Tyndale

MARCH 9—KEEP LOVE BURNING

"And because of the increase of lawlessness,
the love of many will grow cold." Matthew 24:12 NRSV

*W*hen duties of religion are performed in a dead, formal matter, this is a sad symptom of decay in our first love. If the strings of a violin are slack, the violin can never make good music. Believers who grow slack in duty can never make any harmonious sound in God's ears. When spiritual action is slow and the pulse of the soul beats low, it is a sign that Christians have left their first love.

Watch your hearts every day. Take notice of the first declining in love. Observe yourselves when you begin to grow dull and listless, and use all means for quickening. Be much in prayer, meditation, and holy discussion. When the fire is going out, you throw on fuel. So when the flame of your love is going out, make use of gospel principles and promises as fuel to keep the fire of your love burning.

Thomas Watson

Do not lag in zeal, be ardent in spirit, serve the LORD. Romans 12:11 NRSV

*I*f we mean truly to live, we have got to find time for the highest of all exercises, meditation upon the eternal things of God. We have to go to Calvary and reverently contemplate the unveilings of redemptive grace. Love and reverence are not the uncertain products of chance. They are the sure products of thought. If our thought is steadily directed, love and reverence will follow.

Let us go, then, into the school of Calvary with eyes and ears alert and activated that we may see and hear. We shall get into the secret places of the Most High, and we shall observe the unveiling of infinite love. We shall hear that Christian gospel that Pascal heard, and which melted his heart, and hallowed all his years: "I love you more ardently than you have loved your sin."

I know how I have sinned. And, now in the school of Calvary, my Master takes up my passion for sin and contrasts it with His passion for me: "I love you more ardently than you have loved your sin." If in some quiet moment that message swept through our souls in heavenly strains, we should fall in love with the lover.

John Henry Jowett

THE REDEEMER'S AFFECTION—MARCH 11

He who loves his brother abides in the light. 1 John 2:10 NKJV

*T*hrough eternal ages, the Son of God became in the fullness of time the Son of Man. He became the Light of the world as well as the Lamb of God. In each aspect of doing the will as well as the work of God, He thus revealed the wondrous love and grace of the Father and His own perfect Sonship. The Father's will included Christ's glad reception of all who come to Him, His meeting all their needs, saving, sanctifying, satisfying, keeping, raising up at the last day, His giving Himself for, and giving Himself to all those given to Him of the Father.

The Friend who sticks closer than a brother is precious at all times, but never so valued as in times of adversity. The very expression "the Light of the world" tells us of the darkness not only around but also within. The shining of the face of the Son dispels the darkness and the gloom, manifests the presence of the Friend in need, and shows us the Redeemer.

Hudson Taylor

MARCH 12—OUR LOVE

For men shall be lovers of their own selves, covetous, boasters, proud, blasphemers, disobedient to parents, unthankful, unholy. 2 Timothy 3:2 KJV

The love that is in Christ is different from the love that is in us. Love in us is a passion of the soul and, being such, is subject to ebb and flow and be extreme in both ways. For whatever is a passion of the soul, whether love or hatred, joy or fear, is more likely to exceed or come short than to keep within its due bounds. Often that which is loved today is hated tomorrow. Yes, and that which should be loved with bounds of moderation is loved to the drowning of both soul and body in perdition and destruction.

Besides, love in us is likely to choose to itself undue and unlawful objects. Love in us requires that something pleasing and delightful be in the object loved. Love in us decays if the object of our love disappoints our expectation. All this we know to be true. Our love is weak, unorderly, fails and miscarries, either by being too much or too little. The love that is in Christ is not love of the same nature as is love in us. Love in Him is essential to His being.

John Bunyan

MARCH 13—THE MEASURE OF LOVE

As you have heard from the beginning, his command is that you walk in love. 2 John 6 NIV

We must be careful that our love to God is sweet, even, and full of tranquility, having in it no violence. Let our love be prudent and without illusion; that is, that it express itself in such instances which God has chosen or which we choose ourselves by proportion to His rules and measures. Love turns into doting when religion turns into superstition. No degree of love can be imprudent, but the expressions may. We cannot love God too much, but we may proclaim it in an indecent manner.

Let our love be firm, constant, and inseparable. Let it not be coming and returning like the tide, but descending like a never-failing river, ever running into the ocean of divine excellency, passing on in the channels of duty and a constant obedience. Let our love never cease to be what it is until it is turned into sea and vastness, even the immensity of a blessed eternity.

Jeremy Taylor

*He has rescued us from the dominion of darkness
and brought us into the kingdom of the Son he loves. Colossians 1:13 NIV*

*I*t is not surprising that God made such sacrifice to save us. Listen to a humble father as he relates an incident:

My name is Anthony Hunt. About ten years ago, I rode back home after selling cattle in town and buying a doll for Dolly, my little girl. Night set in. A storm that had been brewing broke, and the rain fell in torrents. Suddenly, I heard a little cry, like a child's voice. I couldn't see a thing. Then I became suspicious. I thought it might be a trap. How could a real child be out on the prairie in such a night at such an hour?

Sure enough, I found a little dripping child bundled in wet clothes. I tucked the little soaked child under my coat as best I could. When I arrived home, I saw something was the matter. The room was full of neighbors and my wife amid them weeping.

"Oh, don't tell him," she said. "It will kill him."

"What is it, neighbors?" I cried.

One asked, "What's that in your arms?"

"A poor lost child," I said. "I found it on the road." And I lifted the sleeping child and saw the face of my little Dolly. It was my darling whom I had picked up on the drenched road. My little child had wandered out to meet Papa and the doll while her mother was at work, and for her they were lamenting as for one dead.

S. B. Shaw

Unified Love—March 15

*I have compared thee, O my love, to a company of horses in Pharaoh's chariots.
Song of Solomon 1:9 KJV*

*H*orses originally selected for Pharaoh's own chariot would not only be of the purest blood and perfect in proportion and symmetry, but also perfect in training—docile and obedient. They would know no will but that of the charioteer. The only object of their existence would be to carry the king whithersoever he would go. So should it be with the church of Christ: one body with many members, indwelt and guided by one Spirit, holding the Head, and knowing no will but His.

Hudson Taylor

March 16—Love Is Patient

Charity suffereth long, and is kind. 1 Corinthians 13:4 KJV

*L*ove is long-suffering. If you love your neighbor for God's sake, you will bear long with his shortcomings. If he lacks wisdom, you wilt pity and not despise him. If he is in error, you will mildly try to correct him without any sharpness or reproach. If he is overtaken in a sin, you will labor to restore him in the spirit of meekness. You will have patience with him. God may bring him at length to the knowledge and love of the truth. In all provocations, you will show in yourself a pattern of gentleness and meekness. Let no one deceive you with vain words: He who is not long-suffering has not love.

Love is kind. Whosoever feels the love of God and man in his heart feels an ardent and uninterrupted thirst after the happiness of all his fellow human beings. His soul melts away with the very fervent desire to promote kindness. So that whether he thinks or speaks, or whatever he does, it all points to the same end—the advancing, by every possible way, the happiness of all his fellow human beings. Deceive not your own souls. He who is not kind has not love.

John Wesley

March 17—Growing in Faith

He has showed you, O man, what is good. And what does the LORD require of you?
To act justly and to love mercy and to walk humbly with your God. Micah 6:8 NIV

*G*rowth in the knowledge of God is a condition of growth in His favor. We might grow in knowledge without growing in His favor, because we might not love and trust Him in accordance with the increased knowledge. We cannot love and trust Him more perfectly, unless we become more perfectly acquainted with Him. If our love and faith keep pace with our growing knowledge, we must grow in His favor. But growth in knowledge must be a condition of growth in love and faith.

When we are more and more affected by the mercies of God and by the kindnesses of those around us, when we more thoroughly appreciate manifestations of kindness in God, when we are more and more humbled by these kindnesses and find it more and more natural "to do justly, and to love mercy, and to walk humbly," and live gratefully, we have evidence that we are growing in favor with God.

Charles Finney

If I give away all my possessions. . .but do not have love, I gain nothing.
1 Corinthians 13:3 NRSV

*P*aul contrasts love with other things that people in those days thought much of. He contrasts love with eloquence. What a noble gift it is, the power of playing upon the wills of people and rousing them to lofty purposes. Paul says, "If I speak with the tongues of men and of angels, and have not love, I am become as sounding brass, or a tinkling cymbal." And we all know why. We have all felt the brazenness of words without emotion, and the hollowness of eloquence behind which lies no love.

Love is greater than benevolence. A charitable act is only a little bit of love, one of the innumerable avenues of love, and there may even be, and there is, a great deal of charity without love. It is a very easy thing to toss a coin to a beggar on the street. It is generally an easier thing than not to do it. Yet, love is just as often in the withholding. We purchase relief from the sympathetic feelings roused by the spectacle of misery at the coin's cost. It is too cheap—too cheap for us, and often too dear for the beggar. If we really loved him, we would either do more for him or less.

Henry Drummond

REVITALIZED LOVE—MARCH 19

Consider how I love your precepts; preserve my life according to your steadfast love.
Psalm 119:159 NRSV

*G*od is the chief good, and all our happiness consists in His love. His love should be valued and sought above all things. He is our only Lord, and therefore chiefly to be served. We must love Him with all our heart, soul, and strength. Our great business in the world is to glorify God and obtain salvation. Are these beliefs seen in our practice? Or rather, do our works deny what our words affirm?

But no matter how much our principles inspire us to our work, we are sure we can never do too much. No person can obey or serve God too much. As long as we are swayed by the world, we can never be righteous too much. People of the world think that faithful diligence in the service of Christ is a foolish peculiarity. The time will come when they will easily confess that God could not be loved or served too much and that no one can be too earnest to save his soul. We may easily do too much for the world, but we cannot for God.

Richard Baxter

But I trusted in your steadfast love; my heart shall rejoice in your salvation. Psalm 13:5 NRSV

I was once talking to an intelligent agnostic. He said, "The Christians I meet seem to me to be the very most uncomfortable people anywhere around. They seem to carry their religion as a man carries a headache. He does not want to get rid of his head, but at the same time, it is very uncomfortable to have it."

This was a lesson I have never forgotten. It seemed, as one of my Christian friends said to me one day when we were comparing our experiences, "as if we had just enough religion to make us miserable." The religion of the Lord Jesus Christ was meant to be full of comfort, because "eye has not seen, nor ear heard, neither have entered into the heart of man the things which God has prepared for them that love Him." All the difficulty arises from the fact that we have underbelieved and undertrusted.

Hannah Whitall Smith

MARCH 21—CROSS OF LOVE

"If anyone desires to come after Me, let him deny himself,
and take up his cross daily, and follow Me." Luke 9:23 NKJV

*T*o carry the cross, to love the cross, to chastise the body and bring it to subjection, to flee honors, to endure contempt gladly, to despise self, to suffer any adversity and loss, to desire no prosperous days on earth—this is not man's way. If you rely upon yourself, you can do none of these things, but if you trust in the Lord, strength will be given you from heaven. The world and the flesh will be made subject to your word. You will not even fear your enemy, the devil, if you are armed with faith and signed with the cross of Christ. Set yourself, then, like a good and faithful servant of Christ, to bear bravely the cross of your Lord, who out of love was crucified for you.

Thomas à Kempis

LOVE THE LAW—MARCH 22

Oh, how I love your law! I meditate on it all day long. Psalm 119:97 NIV

gracious soul loves God's laws and is glad of the law because it checks his sinful excesses. The heart would be ready to run wild in sin if it had not some blessed restraints put upon it by the law of God. He who loves God loves His law—the law of repentance, the law of self-denial.

Many say they love God, but they hate His laws. God's precepts are compared to cords: They bind men to their good behavior, but the wicked think these cords too tight; therefore, they say, "Let us break them." They pretend to love Christ as a Savior, but hate Him as a king. Sinners would have Christ put a crown upon their head, but not a yoke upon their neck. He would be a strange king who should rule without laws.

Thomas Watson

LOVE THE BIBLE—MARCH 23

But as it is written, Eye hath not seen, nor ear heard, neither have entered into the heart of man, the things which God hath prepared for them that love him. 1 Corinthians 2:9 KJV

All the historical things are told in the way that we know the world had of looking at them when they were written. People very often think that science is all fact and that religion is only fancy. A great many persons think the stars around us are inhabited, but they cannot bring themselves to believe that there is a life beyond this earth for immortal souls.

The true Christian puts faith before reason and believes that reason always goes wrong when faith is set aside. If people would but read their Bibles more, and study what there is to be found there about heaven, they would not be as worldly minded as they are. They would not have their hearts set upon things down here but would seek the imperishable things above.

Dwight Lyman Moody

March 24—Overwhelmed with Love

And the Word became flesh, and dwelt among us (and we beheld his glory, glory as of the only begotten from the Father), full of grace and truth. John 1:14 ASV

The souls of the saints, when they leave their bodies at death, go to receive a glorious fellowship with Christ. The nature of this glory of Christ will be such as will draw and encourage them. They will not only see infinite majesty and greatness, but infinite grace, mildness, gentleness, and sweetness, all equal to His majesty.

The sight of Christ's great kingly majesty will be no terror to them but will only serve the more to heighten their pleasure and surprise. The souls of departed saints with Christ in heaven shall have Christ manifesting His infinite riches of love toward them. They shall be enabled to express their love to Him, in an infinitely better manner than ever they could while on earth. They shall eat and drink abundantly, swim in the ocean of love, and be eternally swallowed up in the infinitely bright, infinitely mild, and sweet beams of divine love—eternally receiving that light, eternally full of it, and eternally compassed round with it.

Jonathan Edwards

March 25—Love, the Cure for Evil

Be not overcome of evil, but overcome evil with good. Romans 12:21 KJV

He who lives in the purity of love is risen out of the power of evil into the freedom of the one spirit of heaven. The schools have given us very accurate definitions of every vice, whether it be covetousness, pride, wrath, envy, etc. But the Christian has a much shorter way of knowing their nature and power and what they all are and do in and to himself. For call them by what names you will, or distinguish them with ever so much exactness, they are all, separately and jointly, just that same one thing, and all do that same one work. If you would therefore have a true sense of the nature and power of pride, wrath, covetousness, envy, etc., they are in their whole nature nothing else but the murderers and crucifiers of the true Christ of God.

This therefore is a certain truth: That hell and death, curse and misery can never cease or be removed from the Creation till the will of the creature is again as it came from God and is only a spirit of love that wills nothing but goodness.

William Law

Love never fails. 1 Corinthians 13:8 NKJV

Nothing is more valuable and commendable, and yet not one duty is less practiced than that of charity. But before I go any further, I shall inform you what the apostle means by charity, and that is love. If there is true love, there will be charity. There will be an endeavor to assist, help, and relieve according to that ability wherewith God has blessed us.

We often pretend concern for the misery of our fellow-creatures, but yet we seldom commiserate their condition so much as to relieve them according to our abilities. But unless we assist them with what they may stand in need of—for the body as well as for the soul—all our wishes are no more than words of no value. When we hear of any deplorable circumstance in which our fellow-creatures are involved, be they friends or enemies, it is our duty as Christians to assist them to the utmost of our power.

George Whitefield

THE RIGHT CHARITY—MARCH 27

…love one another deeply from the heart. 1 Peter 1:22 NRSV

Your charity is not of the right kind when it proceeds from worldly views. If it is to be seen of men, to receive any advantage from them, to be esteemed or to gain a reputation in the world, then it is all in vain. If you have any pride in it and expect to reap benefits from God merely for it, then it is all in vain. Your charity does not proceed from a right motive, but you are hereby deceiving your own souls. If you give alms purely to be observed by man, then you have not the glory of God or the benefit of your fellow-creatures at heart but merely yourself. This is not charity.

Our charity comes from a right intention when it proceeds from love to God and for the welfare both of the body and soul of our fellow-creatures. When this is the sole end of relieving our distressed fellow-creatures, then our charity comes from a right reason. This is the charity that is pleasing to God. God is well pleased when all our actions proceed from love—love to Himself and love to immortal souls.

George Whitefield

His mouth is most sweet; Yea, he is altogether lovely.
This is my beloved, and this is my friend,
O daughters of Jerusalem. Song of Solomon 5:16 ASV

*G*od is a faithful friend. He is faithful in His love. He gave His very heart to us, when He gave the Son out of His bosom. Here was a pattern of love without a parallel. He is faithful in His promises. He is faithful in His dealings.

God is a permanent friend. Friends often fail at a pinch. Many deal with their friends as women do with flowers; while they are fresh, they put them in their bosoms, but when they begin to wither, they throw them away. Accordingly, if prosperity shine on men, then friends will look upon them. But if there be a cloud of adversity on them, they will not come near them. But God is a friend forever. Although David walked in the shadow of death, he knew he had a friend by him. God, being such a friend, will make all things work for our good. A friend will seek the good of his friend. God never takes off His love wholly from His people.

Thomas Watson

MARCH 29—LOVE THAT ACQUITS

Pursue a godly life, along with faith, love, perseverance, and gentleness.
1 Timothy 6:11 NLT

*J*esus Christ came into the world to save sinners. I know that it is to me even to this day the greatest wonder that I ever heard of, that God should ever justify me. I feel myself to be a lump of unworthiness and a heap of sin apart from His almighty love. I know by a full assurance that I am justified by faith that is in Christ Jesus. Yet, by nature I must take my place among the most sinful. I am loved with as much love as if I had always been godly, although earlier I was ungodly. Who can help being astonished at this? Gratitude for such favor stands dressed in robes of wonder.

The salvation of God is for those who do not deserve it. The Lord only does that which is needful. Infinite wisdom never attempts that which is unnecessary. Jesus never undertakes that which is superfluous. To make him just who is just is no work for God. But to make him just who is unjust—that is work for infinite love and mercy. To justify the ungodly—this is a miracle worthy of God.

Charles Haddon Spurgeon

He looked up, saw Jesus walking nearby, and said,
"Here he is, God's Passover Lamb." John 1:36 TM

*T*here is a happy land, far, far away!" I do not think we greatly help the cause of the Lord by proclaiming the remoteness of His home. I have never been able to find out what we gain by teaching children the "far-offness" of the Savior's dwelling. I am afraid that the remoteness of the home tends to create a conception of the remoteness of the Lover; and, if the Lover is away, the invitation will be very mechanical and cold.

Destroying all sense of remoteness, we must labor to bring the children into the immediate presence of the lover Himself. We have to reveal Jesus to the children, so that He captivates their love. We must strive to make it so real that the children, with their magnificently realistic imagination, shall feel that they are with Him among the flowers of the field. We must reveal Him watching the graceful flight of the birds in the air and His tender regard for the common sparrow. We must reveal Him as the approachable Jesus with groups of little children clustering about His knees and lovingly taking them into His arms to bless them.

John Henry Jowett

Constrained by Love—March 31

"Should you help the wicked and love those who hate the Lord?" 2 Chronicles 19:2 NIV

*B*ecause God loved the world, He gave His well-beloved Son to be both prince and Savior. In knowing, loving, and serving Him, we can realize our supreme blessedness. Is Jesus your King? Never until He is so will you know the fullness of God's love. Those who question or refuse His authority are always in doubt about the love of God to themselves and to the world. Those, on the other hand, who acknowledge His claims and crown Him as King, suddenly find themselves admitted to a standpoint of vision in which doubts and disputations vanish. Then they experience divine love in its most entrancing characteristics. All is love where Jesus reigns.

F. B. Meyer

APRIL 1—SHORT LIFE OF LOVE

He will swallow up death in victory; and the LORD God will
wipe away tears from off all faces. Isaiah 25:8 KJV

I received the following letter from a former orphan on the death of one of his sisters.

"My dear sir," the letter said. "It has pleased the Lord to take unto Himself my dear sister Elizabeth. I had lived in the fond hope of seeing her again, but it was the will of God that it should not be so. I now hope to meet her again with my dear father and mother in that happy land where God shall wipe away all tears from our eyes. It is now plainly to be seen what a mercy it was that we were taken to the orphanage where we all learned to know and love the Savior. It is three years since I left, and I can only say that goodness and mercy have followed me. I often need the help of God to overcome temptations, but in all my failings and wanderings, the hand of God has not suffered me to fall away. I have constant need of prayer."

This was the last letter I had from this lovely youth who gave us great comfort while under our care. He walked as a most consistent Christian for the three years and a half he was employed. I learned from his Christian foreman that he died of typhus fever.

George Müller

APRIL 2—MOLDED IN LOVE

But we know that when he appears, we shall be like him,
for we shall see him as he is. 1 John 3:2 NIV

T he first and chief need of our Christian life is fellowship with God. As I need every moment fresh air to breathe, as the sun every moment sends down its light, so it is only in direct living communication with God that my soul can be strong. Let God's love overwhelm you and bow you still lower down. Sink down before Him in humility, meekness, patience, and surrender to His goodness and mercy. Then accept and value your place in Christ Jesus. He loves you with a personal love. He looks every day for the personal response of your love. Look into His face with trust until His love really shines into your heart. Make His heart glad by telling Him that you do love Him. He offers Himself to you as a personal Savior and keeper from the power of sin.

Andrew Murray

God gave the land of these kings as an inheritance—His faithful love endures forever.
Psalm 136:21 NLT

*D*o you desire one who can love you? None can love you like Christ. His love is incomprehensible; His love passes all other love. The love of the Lord Jesus is first and without beginning; His love is free without any motive; His love is great without any measure; His love is constant without any change; His love is everlasting.

The love of the Lord Jesus Christ brought Him down from heaven and veiled His divinity in a human soul and body. It was love that made Him subject to hunger, thirst, and sorrow. His love carried Him back to heaven that He might make intercession for those whom He had redeemed.

If you have promised yourself to Christ, you will converse with Him. You will endeavor to promote His interest and advance His name in the world. Consider who the Lord Jesus is, whom you are invited to embrace yourselves with. There is none comparable to Jesus Christ.

George Whitefield

Where Love Is—April 4

And I have caused them to dwell, for I have loved them. Zechariah 10:6 YLT

*W*here love is, God is. He who dwells in love dwells in God. God is love. Therefore lavish love upon the poor, where it is very easy. Lavish it especially upon the rich, who often need it most. Lavish love upon our equals, where it is very difficult and for whom perhaps we each do least of all. There is a difference between trying to please and giving pleasure. Lose no chance of giving pleasure. For that is the ceaseless and anonymous triumph of a truly loving spirit.

I shall pass through this world but once. Any good thing, therefore, that I can do or any kindness that I can show to any human being, let me do it now. Love envies not. Whenever you attempt a good work, you will find other people doing the same kind of work and probably doing it better. Envy them not. Envy is a feeling of ill will to those who are in the same line as ourselves. That most despicable of all the unworthy moods that clouds a Christian's soul assuredly waits for us on the threshold of every work unless we are fortified with this grace of generosity of spirit.

Henry Drummond

APRIL 5—MOTHER'S LOVE

"How often I have longed to gather your children together." Matthew 23:37 NIV

What a mother does for her foolish, careless, ignorant, but dearly loved little ones, this very thing our God does for us. When a mother is with her children, she thinks of their comfort and well-being always before her own. They must have comfortable seats where no cold air can reach them, no matter what amount of discomfort she may be compelled to endure. Their beds must be soft and their blankets warm; let hers be what they may. Their paths must be smooth and safe, although she is obliged to walk in rough and dangerous ways. Her own comfort, as compared with that of her children, is of no account in a loving mother's eyes. Surely our God has not made the mothers in this world more capable of a self-sacrificing love than He is Himself. He must be better and greater in love and self-sacrifice than any mother He ever made.

Hannah Whitall Smith

APRIL 6—CHRISTLIKE LOVE

I pray that. . .Christ may dwell in your hearts through faith. Ephesians 3:16–17 NIV

A minister's wife told me that at one time they had moved to a new place. Her little boy came in after the first afternoon of play. He exclaimed joyfully, "Mother, I have found such a lovely, good little girl to play with that I never want to go away again."

"I am very glad, darling," said the loving mother, delighted because of her child's happiness. "What is the little girl's name?"

The child replied with a sudden solemnity, "I think her name is Jesus."

"Frank!" exclaimed the mother. "What do you mean?"

He said deprecatingly, "She was so lovely that I did not know what she could be called but Jesus."

Are our lives so Christlike that anyone could have such a thought of us? Is it apparent to all around us that we have been with Jesus? Unfortunately, it is often just the contrary. Are some of us so cross and uncomfortable in our living that exactly the opposite thing would have to be said about us?

Hannah Whitall Smith

"So, because you are lukewarm—neither hot nor cold—
I am about to spit you out of my mouth." Revelation 3:16 NIV

*O*ur love to God is sincere when it is pure and without self-interest. We must love Christ for Himself. God's beauty and love must be the two loadstones to draw our love to Him. Alexander the Great had two friends, Hephestion and Craterus, of whom he said, "Hephestion loves me because I am Alexander; Craterus loves me because I am King Alexander." The one loved his person; the other loved his gifts. We must love God more for what He is than for what He bestows. True love is not mercenary. You need not hire a mother to love her child. A soul deeply in love with God needs not be hired by rewards. It cannot but love Him for that luster of beauty that sparkles forth in Him.

Our love to God must be a fervent love. Saints must be burning in holy love. To love coldly is the same as not to love. The sun shines as hot as it can. Our love to God must be intense and ablaze like coals of juniper. Our love to God must flame forth.

Thomas Watson

ABUSE OF LOVE—APRIL 8

I am shocked that you are turning away so soon from God.
Galatians 1:6 NLT

*T*ake heed of abusing the love of God. This exhortation seems needless because love is such a thing that one would think none could find in their heart to abuse. But I am of opinion that nothing is more abused among believers this day than the love of God.

But I say, let not this love of God and of Christ be abused. It is unnatural to abuse love. To abuse love is a villainy condemned of all. Yes, to abuse love is the most inexcusable sin of all. It is the sin of devils to abuse the love of God and of Christ. And what can one say for himself in the judgment who is charged with the abuse of love? Christians, deny yourselves, your lusts, and the vanities of this present life. Devote yourselves to God. Become lovers of God and lovers of His ways. Then shall you show to all people that you have not received the grace of God in vain.

John Bunyan

They placed their hope in the resurrection to a better life. Hebrews 11:35 NLT

*I*did everything I could to bring him to Christ. He was a young man of considerable promise. But day by day, I preached to him as best I knew how. I think I never loved a man on earth as I loved that brother. Because he was sickly, that drew my love and sympathy toward him. How my heart yearned for his salvation!

After preaching one night, I said, "Now if any of this audience would like to take up his cross and follow Christ, I would like for him to rise." I cannot tell you what a thrill of joy filled my soul when that brother of mine arose! It seemed the happiest night of my life. I was full of joy and thankfulness. Afterward this brother and I worked together for a time.

After a year had passed, I went to Chicago. He was to come later. He bid me good-bye, and I said, "Samuel, I will see you in a few days, so I will only say good-bye till then." A few days after, a telegram came, saying, "Samuel is dead." I got more comfort out of that promise "I will raise him up at the last day" than anything else in the Bible. How it cheered me! How it lighted up my path!

Dwight Lyman Moody

"Simon son of John, do you truly love me more than these?" John 21:15 NIV

*W*hatever you love more than God is your idol. Rich and poor, learned and unlearned, all classes of men and women are guilty of this sin. A man may make a god of some precious gift that God has bestowed upon him.

Many make a god of pleasure. If some old Greek or Roman came to life again and saw man in a drunken display, would he believe that the worship of Bacchus had died out? If he saw the streets of our large cities filled with prostitutes, would he believe that the worship of Venus had ceased? Others take fashion as their god. They give their time and thought to dress. Do not let us flatter ourselves to think that all idolaters are in heathen countries.

The atheist says that he does not believe in God. He denies His existence, but he can't help setting up some other god in His place. Has the human heart ever been satisfied with these false gods? What do they look forward to? Nothing!

Dwight Lyman Moody

Who shall separate us from the love of Christ? Romans 8:35 NIV

*L*ove is insurmountable when it cannot be overcome with any other love, trial, or temptation—when it gladly casts down all other hindrances and all temptations, and quenches fleshly desires. When a person suffers gladly and submissively all anguish for Christ, and is not overcome with any delight or flattering—so that whether you are in ease or in anguish, in sickness or in health, you would not for all the world anger God at any time—that is insurmountable love. And blessed is the soul that is in this state. Every labor is light to him who loves truly; neither can any man better overcome labor than by love.

Therefore take on love as the iron takes on the redness of fire, as air takes in the sun, as the wool absorbs the dye. The coal heats the iron in the fire so it is all fire. The air is infused by the sun so that it is all light. The wool takes the hue so that it changes all to the color.

John Wycliffe

LOVE AND GRATITUDE—APRIL 12

Because he turned his ear to me, I will call on him as long as I live. Psalm 116:1–2 NIV

*T*hanksgiving is just what the word itself signifies—the giving of thanks to God. It is giving something to God in words that we feel in our hearts for blessings received. Gratitude arises from serious meditation on the goodness of God. Both gratitude and thanksgiving have to do with God and His mercies. The heart is consciously grateful to God. The soul gives expression to that heartfelt gratitude to God in words or acts. Gratitude is born of meditation on God's grace and mercy. Herein we see the value of serious meditation. Praise is begotten by gratitude and a conscious obligation to God for mercies given. As we think of mercies past, the heart is inwardly moved to gratitude.

Love is the child of gratitude. Love grows as gratitude is felt and then breaks out into praise and thanksgiving to God. Answered prayers cause gratitude, and gratitude brings forth a love that declares it will not cease praying. Gratitude and love move us to increased praying.

Edward McKendree Bounds

"Father, I want those you have given me to be with me where I am." John 17:24 NIV

When the souls of the saints leave their bodies to go to be with Christ, they see His glory, the beauty of His perfection, His great majesty and almighty power, and His infinite wisdom, holiness, and grace. They see in a much clearer manner than the saints do here what is the length, depth, and height of the grace and love of Christ.

As they see the unspeakable riches and glory of the attribute of God's grace, so they most clearly see and understand Christ's eternal and unmeasurable dying love to them in particular. They see all of this in the most clear and glorious manner, without any darkness or delusion, without any impediment or interruption.

Now the saints while in the body see something of Christ's glory and love, as we in the dawning of the morning see something of the reflected light of the sun mingled with darkness. But when separated from the body, they see their glorious and loving Redeemer, as we see the sun when risen, and showing its whole disk above the horizon in a clear hemisphere and with perfect day.

Jonathan Edwards

APRIL 14—BESET WITH LOVE

Thou hast beset me behind and before, and laid thine hand upon me. Psalm 139:5 KJV

Some of us know what it is to be intruded upon by unwelcome and unpleasant people. Perhaps we never have thought that God besets us. He loves us so that He cannot leave us alone. Neither coldness nor rebuffs on our part can drive Him away. Yes, it is gloriously true!

Moreover, He besets us behind as well as before, just as a mother does. She goes after her children and picks up all they have dropped, and clears away all the litter they have left behind them. We mothers begin this in the nursery with the blocks and playthings, and we go on with it all our lives long. We are seeking continually to set straight that which our children have left crooked behind them. Often it is at the cost of much toil and trouble, but always with a love that makes the toil and trouble nothing in comparison to caring for the children we love.

All this and more does our God do for us from our earliest infancy, long even before we know enough to be conscious of it, until the very end of our earthly lives.

Hannah Whitall Smith

No one has ever seen God. 1 John 4:12 NIV

*I*f we consider how little each one of us practices brotherly love, we shall rightly be ashamed of our negligence. Daily God declares Himself reconciled to us in His Son. Christ bears witness in this law of love that He is the giver of peace with God. He offers Himself for us, so that we may willingly be brothers to one another. We desire indeed to be enrolled as children of God and to enjoy the reconciliation won for us by the blood of Christ. Meanwhile we tear at one another; we sharpen our teeth; our minds are wholly ruthless. If we wish to prove ourselves disciples of Christ, we must heed this part of His teaching, and each one of us strive to help his neighbors.

This cannot be done without opposition from the flesh. We are prone to love ourselves and to seek too much our own private advantage. We must shed these immoderate and hurtful emotions of self-interest if brotherly love is to take their place. We are warned in scripture that it is not enough to refrain from doing injury; a man must be helpful to his brothers.

John Calvin

The Strength for Love—April 16

I love you, O Lord, my strength.
Psalm 18:1 NRSV

*T*he law requires a free, a willing, and a loving heart. I may of my own strength refrain from hurting my enemy, but to love him with all my heart and put anger out of my mind, I cannot do of my own strength. I may refuse money of my own strength, but to put away love for riches out of my heart, I cannot do of my own strength. To abstain from adultery, as concerning the outward deed, I can do of my own strength; but not to desire in my heart is as impossible to me as to choose whether I will hunger or thirst. Yet the law requires it. Of our own strength the law is never fulfilled. We must have God's favor and His Spirit, purchased by Christ's blood.

William Tyndale

April 17—The Face of Love

Let your face shine on your servant; save me in your unfailing love. Psalm 31:16 NIV

It is the purpose of God that the heart of Christ shall be revealed to His people. It is the will of God that "the light of the knowledge of the glory of God" should be revealed to us "in the face of Jesus Christ."

How well we know in actual life what the light of the countenance means! How the mother's smile brings light and gladness into the heart of the child! How the welcoming look of a friend is at once understood!

Where there is the shining of the face, we know there is more than forgiveness. There is favor and disposition to please. What a wonderful view of the light of His countenance the favored disciples must have had who were witnesses of His transfiguration. We are told that His face did shine as the sun. And so when the Lord makes the light of His countenance to shine upon any of His people, in the measure in which with unveiled face they discern the beauty of the Lord, there is a moral and progressive change into His likeness.

Hudson Taylor

April 18—Love the Good Seed

*"I said, 'Plant the good seeds of righteousness, and you will harvest a crop of my love.'"
Hosea 10:12 NLT*

Protestant missionaries of every denomination in South Africa all agree in one point, that no mere profession of Christianity is sufficient to entitle the converts to the Christian name. They are all anxious to place the Bible in the hands of the natives. With the ability to read that, there can be little doubt as to the future. We believe Christianity to be divine and equal to all it has to perform. Let the good seed be widely sown, and no matter to what sect the converts may belong, the harvest will be glorious.

Let nothing that I have said be interpreted as indicative of feelings unfavorable to any body of Christians, for I never, as a missionary, felt myself to be either Presbyterian, Episcopalian, or Independent, or called upon in any way to love one denomination less than another. My earnest desire is that those who really have the best interests of the heathen at heart should go to them. Assuredly, in Africa at least, self-denying labors among real heathen will not fail to be appreciated. Christians have never yet been disappointed in dealing fairly with the heathen.

David Livingstone

...for ye yourselves are taught of God to love one another. 1 Thessalonians 4:9 KJV

I cannot see God, but as a compensation I can see my brother. If I love him, God dwells in me. Loving my brother is the way to real fellowship with God. Suppose there is a brother, a most unlovable man. He worries you every time you meet him. He is of the very opposite disposition to yours. You have to deal with him in your business. He is most untidy and unbusinesslike. You say, "I cannot love him." Friend, you have not learned the lesson that Christ wanted to teach above everything. Let a man be what he will, you are to love him. Yes, listen! If a man loves not his brother whom he hath seen—if you don't love that unlovable man whom you have seen—how can you love God whom you have not seen? If the love of God is in your heart, you will love your brother.

Andrew Murray

GENTLE LOVE—APRIL 20

What do you prefer? Shall I come to you with a whip,
or in love and with a gentle spirit? 1 Corinthians 4:21 NIV

*T*he apostle earnestly sought the Corinthian converts by the gentleness of Christ. Although there were abuses amongst them that seemed to call for stringent dealing, he felt that the abuses could be best removed by the gentle love that he had learned from the heart of Christ. The wisdom that is from above is gentle as well as pure.

In dealing with the sin that chokes our growth, it is probable that gentleness will do more than severity. The gentleness is the furnace before which the foul ingredients of our hearts are driven out never to return. We might challenge the lion, but we are conquered by the Lamb. We could withstand the scathing look of scorn, but when the gentle Lord casts on us the look of inexpressible tenderness, we go out to weep bitterly.

He has borne with us so lovingly. He has filled our lives with mercy even when compelled to correct. He has returned our rebuffs and slights with meekness and forbearance. He has never wearied of us. This is an everlasting tribute to the gentleness that makes great.

F. B. Meyer

April 21—Love Is Not Prideful

But let those who boast boast in this, that they understand and know me,
that I am the LORD; I act with steadfast love, justice, and righteousness in the earth.
Jeremiah 9:24 NRSV

*I*f you love your neighbor as yourself, you will not be able to prefer yourself before him. You will not be able to despise anyone, any more than to hate him. As the wax melts away before the fire, so does pride melt away before love. All haughtiness, whether of heart, speech, or behavior, vanishes away where love prevails. It brings down the high looks of him who boasts in his strength and makes him as a little child—humble of himself, willing to hear, glad to learn, easily convinced, easily persuaded. And whoever is otherwise minded, let him give up all vain hope: He is puffed up and so has not love.

Whatever we do and whatever we suffer, if we are not renewed in the spirit of our mind by the love of God shed in our hearts by the Holy Ghost, we cannot enter into life eternal.

John Wesley

April 22—Love Across the Ages

"For God so loved the world, that he gave his only begotten Son, that whosoever
believeth in him should not perish, but have everlasting life." John 3:16 KJV

*L*ong before God formed a moral universe, He knew perfectly what it must cost Him to redeem sinners, and He knew that the result would amply justify all the cost. He knew that a wonder of mercy would be wrought—that the suffering demanded of Christ, great as it was, would be endured—and that results infinitely glorious would accrue therefrom.

He looked down the track of time into the distant ages—where there might be seen the joys of redeemed saints, who are singing their songs and striking their harps anew with the everlasting song, and was not this enough for the heart of infinite love to enjoy?

When you come to see Him face-to-face and tell Him what you think of it—when you are some thousands of years older than you are now—will you not adore that wisdom that manages this scheme, and the infinite love in which it had its birth?

Charles Finney

But the stranger that dwelleth with you shall be unto you as one born among you, and thou shalt love him as thyself. Leviticus 19:34 KJV

Consider what Christ did toward the saving of souls. He thought them worth His blood. Shall we not think them worth our breath? Will you not do a little where Christ has done so much? Consider what fit objects of concern ungodly people are to us. They are dead in trespasses and sins and have not hearts to feel their miseries or to regret their own condition. If others do not take pity on them, they will have no pity. It is the nature of their disease to make them pitiless to themselves. Yes, they are their own most cruel destroyers.

This is the misery of man's nature: Though every man naturally hates sorrow and loves the most merry and joyful life, yet few love the way to joy or will endure the pains by which it is obtained. They will be content with earthly pleasures rather than ascend to heaven to seek a joyful life.

Richard Baxter

TRUSTING LOVE—APRIL 24

" I will save my flock, and they will no longer be plundered. I will place over them one shepherd, my servant David, and he will tend them; he will tend them and be their shepherd.'" Ezekiel 34:22–23 NIV

Centuries before Jesus came to be the shepherd, the Father said: "And I will set up one shepherd over them, and He shall feed them." I catch a glimpse of the Father's yearning love as I read these words. None therefore who are in this flock need fear any evil.

If our faith will but claim Him in this blessed and wondrous relationship, He will care for us according to His love, His wisdom, and His power, and not according to our poor comprehension of it. Enter into this relationship with Christ and really be a helpless, docile, trusting sheep, and believe Him to be your shepherd with all the love, care, and tenderness that that name involves. If you will follow Him wherever He leads, you will soon lose all your old spiritual discomfort, and will know the peace of God that passes all understanding to keep your hearts and minds in Christ Jesus.

Hannah Whitall Smith

"Everyone on the side of truth listens to me." John 18:37 NIV

*T*ruth, not eloquence, is to be sought in reading the holy scriptures. Every part must be read in the spirit in which it was written. For in the scriptures we ought to seek profit rather than polished diction.

Likewise, we ought to read simple and devout books as willingly as learned and profound ones. We ought not to be swayed by the authority of the writer, whether he be a great literary light or an insignificant person, but by the love of simple truth. We ought not to ask who is speaking but mark what is said. Men pass away, but the truth of the Lord remains forever. God speaks to us in many ways without regard for persons.

O Lord, let Your truth teach me. Let it guard me, and keep me safe to the end. Let it free me from all evil affection and badly ordered love, and I shall walk with You in great freedom of heart.

Thomas à Kempis

APRIL 26—INTERCEDE IN LOVE

I exhort therefore, first of all, that supplications, prayers, intercessions, thanksgivings, be made for all men. 1 Timothy 2:1 ASV

*S*ome forget this duty of praying for others because they seldom remember to pray for themselves. Even those who are constant in praying to their Father are often so selfish in their addresses that they do not enlarge their petitions for the welfare of their fellow Christians.

Intercession will fill your hearts with love one to another. He who every day heartily intercedes at the throne of grace for all mankind cannot but in a short time be filled with love and charity to all. The frequent exercise of his love in this manner will gradually enlarge his heart. He will be filled with joy, peace, meekness, long-suffering, and all other graces of the Holy Spirit. By frequently laying his neighbor's wants before God, he will be touched with a fellow-feeling for them. Every blessing bestowed on others, instead of exciting envy in him, will be looked on as an answer to his particular intercession and fill his soul with joy unspeakable and full of glory.

George Whitefield

The Lord is gracious and merciful, slow to anger and abounding in steadfast love.
Psalm 145:8 NRSV

No form of vice, not worldliness, not greed of gold, not drunkenness itself, does more to unChristianize society than evil temper. For embittering life, for breaking up communities, for destroying the most sacred relationships, for devastating homes, for withering up men and women; in short, for sheer gratuitous misery-producing power, this influence stands alone.

Ill temper is not in what it is alone, but in what it reveals. It is a test for love, a symptom, a revelation of an unloving nature. It is not enough to deal with the temper. We must go to the source and change the inmost nature. Souls are made sweet not by taking the acid fluids out but by putting something in—a great love. The spirit of Christ penetrating our spirits, sweetens, purifies, and transforms all.

Henry Drummond

God Is Life—April 28

You have granted me life and steadfast love, and your care has preserved my spirit.
Job 10:12 NRSV

Now, nothing wills and works with God but the spirit of love because nothing else works in God Himself. The Almighty brought forth all nature for this only end that boundless love might have its infinity of height and depth to dwell and work in. All the striving and working properties of nature are only to give essence and substance, life and strength to the invisible hidden spirit of love, that it may come forth into outward activity and manifest its blessed powers, that creatures born in the strength and out of the powers of nature might communicate the spirit of love and goodness, give and receive mutual delight and joy to and from one another.

William Law

You must have accurate and honest weights and measures. Deuteronomy 25:15 NIV

What would Jesus do in Milton Wright's place as a businessman?

He would engage in the business first of all for the purpose of glorifying God, and not for the primary purpose of making money. All money that might be made He would never regard as His own, but as trust funds to be used for the good of humanity. His relations with all the persons in His employ would be the most loving and helpful. He could not help but think of all of them in the light of souls to be saved. This thought would always be greater than His thought of making money in the business. He would never do a single dishonest or questionable thing or try in any remote way to get the advantage of anyone else in the same business.

The principles of unselfishness and helpfulness in the business would direct all its details. He would shape the entire plan of His relations to His employees, to the people who were His customers, and to the general business world with which He was connected.

Milton Wright said, "Intelligent unselfishness ought to be wiser than intelligent selfishness. I am absolutely convinced that Jesus in my place would be absolutely unselfish. He would love all these men in His employ. He would consider the main purpose of all the business to be a mutual helpfulness and would conduct it all so that God's kingdom would be evidently the first object sought."

Charles Sheldon

APRIL 30—EMBRACE HIS LOVE

Steadfast love and faithfulness will meet. Psalm 85:10 NRSV

Some of us know what it is to love, and we know that if we could only have our way, our beloved ones would be overwhelmed with blessings. All that is good and sweet and lovely in life would be poured out upon them from our lavish hands, had we but the power to carry out our will for them. And if this is the way of love with us, how much more must it be so with our God, who is love itself. If we could but get a glimpse into the mighty depths of His love, our hearts would spring out to meet His will and embrace it as our richest treasure. We would abandon ourselves to it with an enthusiasm of gratitude and joy that such a wondrous privilege could be ours.

Hannah Whitall Smith

My purpose is that they may be encouraged in heart and united in love, so that they may have the full riches of complete understanding. Colossians 2:2 NIV

I have learned that when anyone becomes in earnest about his soul's salvation, and he begins to seek God, it does not take long for an anxious sinner to meet an anxious Savior. Those who seek for Him with all their hearts find Christ.

I believe the reason why so few find Christ is that they do not search for Him with all their hearts. Everything God has done proves that He is in earnest about the salvation of men's souls. And the Lord wants us to be in earnest when it comes to this great question of the soul's salvation. I never saw men seeking Him with all their hearts but they soon found Him.

It was quite refreshing one night to find a young man who thought he was not worth saving, he was so vile and wicked. There was hope for him because he was so desperately in earnest about his soul. He had a sight of himself in God's looking glass and had a very poor opinion of himself. But the moment he sees God by the eye of faith, he is down on his knees, and, like Job, he cries, "Behold, I am vile."

Dwight Lyman Moody

LOVING THOUGHTS—MAY 2

I hate vain thoughts: but thy law do I love. Psalm 119:113 KJV

This is the language of a gracious spirit: "My God sees what a hard heart I have; therefore, He drives in one wedge of trial after another to break my heart. He knows how I am full of bad temper, how sick of a disease; therefore, He cleanses by blood to save my life. This severe action is either to restrain some vice or to exercise some grace. How good is God who will not let me alone in my sins, but smites my body to save my soul!" In this way, he who loves God takes everything with a good attitude.

Love puts a glowing interpretation upon all God's actions. You who are prone to murmur at God, as if He had dealt ill with you, be humbled for this. Say to yourself, "If I loved God more, I should have better thoughts of God." It is Satan who makes us have good thoughts of ourselves and hard thoughts of God. Love takes all in the fairest sense; it thinks no evil.

Thomas Watson

"Who is like you, O LORD, among the gods? Who is like you, majestic in holiness, awesome in splendor, doing wonders?" Exodus 15:11 NRSV

*L*ove is the greatest thing that God can give us, and it is the greatest thing we can give to God. It is the old; it is the new; it is the great commandment; it is all the commandments. The consideration of God's goodness and bounty are most commonly the first motive of our love. But when we are once entered and have tasted the goodness of God, we love the source for its own excellence.

Love does all things that may please the beloved person. Love is obedient. Love gives away all things to advance the interest of the beloved person. Love is always liberal and expressive. It suffers all things that are imposed by its beloved. Love is patient and content with anything, provided it can be with its beloved. Love is also impatient of anything that may displease the beloved person. Love is not divided between God and God's enemy. We must love God with all our heart; that is, give Him a whole and undivided affection, having love for nothing else but such things which He allows, and which He commands or loves Himself.

Jeremy Taylor

MAY 4—GRACIOUS LOVE

The LORD is compassionate and gracious, slow to anger, abounding in love. Psalm 103:8 NIV

*H*ad God told us that He was not gracious, that He took no interest in our welfare, and that He had no intention of pardoning us, we could have no peace and no hope. In that case, our knowing God would only make us miserable. For how fearful a thing must it be to have the great God who made us, the great Father of Spirits, against us and not for us!

Strange to say, this is the very state of anxiety in which we may find many who profess to believe in God! With the Bible in their hands and the cross before their eyes, they wander on in a state of darkness and fear, such as would have arisen had God revealed Himself in hatred, not in love. Have they misunderstood the Bible? Have they mistaken the character of God, looking on Him as an austere man and a hard master?

But God has declared Himself gracious. God is love. The more, then, that we know of this God and of His grace, the more will His peace fill us.

Horatius Bonar

*Each of you must give as you have made up your mind not reluctantly
or under compulsion, for God loves a cheerful giver. 2 Corinthians 9:7 NRSV*

*I*f you know the love of Jesus as the deer thirsts for the brooks, so will you desire greater portions of His love. If you do not desire to know Him better, then you do not love Him because love always cries, "Nearer, nearer." Only be content with an increasing acquaintance with Jesus. Seek to know more of Him in His divine nature, in His human relationship, in His finished work, in His death, in His resurrection, in His present glorious intercession, and in His future royal appearance. An increase of love to Jesus and a better understanding of His love to us is one of the best tests of growth in grace.

Our God requires no slaves to adorn His throne. He is the Lord of the empire of love and would have His servants dressed in the uniform of joy. If He sees that we serve Him from force and not because we love Him, He will reject our offering. Take away joyful willingness from the Christian, and you have removed the test of his sincerity. In the joy of the Lord, we are strong.

Charles Haddon Spurgeon

DEEPER LOVE—MAY 6

*Continue your love to those who know you, your righteousness to the upright in heart.
Psalm 36:10 NIV*

*J*esus says, "As the Father has loved Me, so have I loved You: Continue in My love." There is much more to this statement than is commonly believed. It was Christ's purpose to deposit in our laps a sure pledge of God's love toward us. The love in question here has to do with us because it is as the head of the church that Christ testifies to God's love for Him. Let us fix our eyes on Christ because in Him we see the pledge of God's love clearly exhibited. God poured His love upon Him so that it might flow from Him to the members of His body. This is also the significance of the title "the beloved Son, in whom the will of the Father is satisfied." We must consider the purpose of this love, which is that God in Christ may be well pleased with us. Christ was loved by the Father not in and for Himself alone, but that He might with Himself unite us with the Father.

John Calvin

MAY 7—LIVE IN LOVE

"If you obey my commands, you will remain in my love." John 15:10 NIV

*T*he love of the Father to the Son is not a sentiment—it is a divine life, an infinite energy, an irresistible power. It carried Christ through life, death, and the grave. The Father loved Him, dwelt in Him, and did all for Him. So the love of Christ to us, too, is an infinite living power that will work in us. The feebleness of our Christian life is that we do not take time to believe that this divine love does really delight in us, and will possess and work all in us.

Turn away from the visible if you would see and possess the invisible. Turn away from yourself and your efforts if you would have your heart filled with Him and the certainty of His love. Come away from all else, and set your heart on Jesus and His love. Occupy yourself with that love, worship it, and wait for it. You may be sure it will reach out to you and by its power take you up into itself as your home.

Andrew Murray

MAY 8—STEPPING-STONES OF LOVE

"Indeed, you love the people; all your holy ones are in your hands.
They follow in your steps and accept your instruction." Deuteronomy 33:3 NLT

*I*t is a fact that God loves each of us with the tenderest and most special love. You may not believe or feel it. The warm summer sun may be shining against your shuttered and curtained window without making itself seen or felt within. Your failure to realize and appreciate the fact of God's love toward you cannot alter it being so.

After the peace was signed between the North and the South in the great American Civil War, there were soldiers hiding in the woods and starving on berries who might have returned to their homes. They either did not know or did not credit the Good News. They went on starving long after their comrades had been welcomed by their wives and children. Theirs was the loss, but their failure in knowledge or belief did not alter the fact that peace was proclaimed and that the door was wide open for their return.

F. B. Meyer

Whoever lives in love lives in God, and God in him.
1 John 4:16 NIV

When Mr. Moody organized the church in Chicago, he was eager that everybody should always hear this one truth that God is love. He had it put on the gas jets right above the pulpit. The first thing you would see when you went in there on an evening was that text shining out in letters of fire.

One stormy night, before the time of the meeting, the door stood ajar. A man partly intoxicated saw it open and thought he might go in and get warm. When he pushed the door open, he saw the text blazing out, "God is love."

He pulled the door closed and walked away muttering to himself. He said, "God is not love. If God were love, He would love me. God does not love a wretch like me." But it kept on burning down into his soul, "God is love! God is love! God is love!" After a while he retraced his steps and took a seat in a corner.

When Mr. Moody walked down after the meeting, he found the man weeping like a child. "What is the trouble?" Mr. Moody asked. "What was it in the sermon that touched you?"

"I didn't hear a word of your sermon," the man said. "It is the text up there."

Mr. Moody sat down and from his Bible showed him the way of life, and he was saved.

Reuben Archer Torrey

Saul and Jonathan were lovely and pleasant in their lives. 2 Samuel 1:23 KJV

*I*t was very lovely and pleasant of David to speak favorably of Saul and Jonathan. David had no hesitation in saying this of his beloved Jonathan, every memory of whom was very pleasant. But he might have been excused for omitting Saul from the generous description he heaped on the kindred soul of his friend. But death had obliterated the sad, dark memories of recent days. Time had transported the psalmist across the dream of years to Saul as he was when David was first introduced to him.

This is the love of God, which He breathes into the hearts of His children. They become perfect in love, as He is. It is Godlike for His children to love their enemies, bless those who curse them, and pray for all who despitefully use and persecute them. Is such love ours? Do we forbear from thinking evil? Do we look on the virtues more often than the failures of our friends? Do we cast the mantle of forgiveness over the injuries done to us and dwell tenderly on the excellencies of our foes? Such is the love that never fails but endures when faith has turned to fruition, and hope has realized its dreams.

We need most of all a baptism of love. A piece of clay will become fragrant if placed near the fragrance of roses. Let us lie where John did, on the bosom of incarnate love, until we begin to love as he did.

F. B. Meyer

Inasmuch as ye did it unto one of these my brethren. . .ye did it unto me. Matthew 25:40 ASV

*W*hat difference is there between the king on the throne and the beggar on the dunghill when God demands their breaths? There is no difference, my brethren, in the grave, nor will there be any at the Day of Judgment. You will not be excused because you have had a great estate, a fine house, and lived in all the pleasures that earth could afford you. Neither will you be judged according to the largeness of your estate but according to the use you have made of it.

Let me beseech you, my rich brethren, to consider the poor of the world, and how commendable and praiseworthy it is to relieve those who are distressed. Consider how pleasing this is to God, how delightful it is to man, and how many prayers you will have put up for your welfare by those persons whom you relieve. God has blessed you for the relief of His poor.

George Whitefield

Pure religion and undefiled before God and the Father is this, to visit the fatherless and widows in their affliction, and to keep himself unspotted from the world. James 1:27 KJV

I exhort you who are poor to be charitable to one another. You may not have money or the things of this life to bestow upon one another. Yet you may assist them, by comforting and advising them not to be discouraged, though they are low in the world. In sickness you may help them according as you have time or ability. Do not be unkind to one another. Do not grieve or vex or be angry with each other, for this is giving the world an advantage over you.

And if God stirs up any to relieve you, do not make an ill use of what His providence by the hands of some Christian hath bestowed upon you. Be always humble and wait on God. Do not murmur or brood if you see any relieved and you are not. Wait on the Lord, and help one another according to your abilities from time to time.

George Whitefield

OBLIGATION TO LOVE—MAY 13

"Since you are precious and honored in my sight, and because I love you, I will give men in exchange for you, and people in exchange for your life." Isaiah 43:4 NIV

G od is a being infinitely lovely. He has infinite excellency and beauty. He is a being of infinite greatness, majesty, and glory; therefore, He is infinitely honorable. He is infinitely exalted above the greatest kings of the earth, and therefore He is infinitely more honorable than they. He is infinitely worthy to be obeyed Himself, and we have an absolute, universal, and infinite dependence upon Him.

You lived such a wicked life; it would have been most just with God to cast you off. But He has had mercy upon you. He made His glorious grace appear for your everlasting salvation. You had no love for God; yet He exercised unspeakable love to you. So great a value has God's grace set on you that you have been redeemed at the price of the blood of His own Son. God hath made you a joint heir with Christ of His glory. You were ungrateful for past mercies; yet God not only continued those mercies but bestowed unspeakably greater mercies upon you.

Jonathan Edwards

"With unfailing love you will lead this people whom you have ransomed." Exodus 15:13 NLT

You must remember that our God has all knowledge and all wisdom. He may guide you into paths wherein He knows great blessings are awaiting you. But to the shortsighted human eyes around you, the paths may seem sure to result in loss. You must recognize that He knows the end of things from the beginning. He alone can judge what the results of any course of action may be. You must realize that His very love for you may lead you to run counter to the loving wishes of even your dearest friends.

You may be called upon to turn your back on father or mother or husband or wife. The child of God who enters upon this life of obedience is sooner or later led into paths which meet with the disapproval of those he best loves. Unless he is prepared for this and can trust the Lord through it all, he will scarcely know what to do.

The nearer we are to Christ, the more shall we be enabled to show by example the meekness and gentleness of our Lord. The more tender will be our consideration for those who are our natural guardians and counselors. If in obedience to Him we are led to act contrary to the wishes of our friends, we shall prove that His will is our motive by the love and patience that marks our conduct toward them.

Hannah Whitall Smith

MAY 15—POLISHED WITH LOVE

Listen, my child. . . . Don't neglect your mother's teaching. Proverbs 1:8 NLT

I thank God for what mothers' love has done for the world. Surely as Moses was put in his mother's arms by the Egyptian princess, so God has put the babes in your arms as a charge by Him to raise and care for. Every child is put in a mother's arms as a responsibility from God. She has to answer to God for the way she deals with that child. That babe is put in your arms to train for the Lord. No mother has any more right to raise her children for materialism than I have to pick your pockets. She has no more right to do that than a bank cashier has to take the savings of the people.

One of the worst sins you can commit is to be unfaithful to your trust. That child is a jewel that belongs to God, and He gives it to you to polish for Him. Will you promise that from now on you will try, with God's help, to do better than you ever have done to raise your children for God?

Billy Sunday

Place me like a seal over your heart, like a seal on your arm; for love is as strong as death, its jealousy unyielding as the grave. Song of Songs 8:6 NIV

Love to God must be active. Love is no idle ornament. It sets the head studying for God and the feet running in the ways of His commandments. Pretenses of love are insufficient. Love has not only a smooth tongue but also a kind heart. He will be eyes to the blind and feet to the lame. The bellies of the poor shall be where he sows the golden seeds of liberality. Some say they love God, but their love is lame because they give nothing to good uses. Indeed, faith deals with invisibles, but God hates that love which is invisible. Love vents itself in good works.

He who is a lover of God gives Him such a love as he bestows upon none else. Love to God is permanent. Love is like the pulse of the body, always beating. It is not a desert but a spring flood. Nothing can hinder a Christian's love to God. Nothing can conquer love, not any difficulties or oppositions. Neither the sweet waters of pleasure nor the bitter waters of persecution can quench love. Love to God abides firm to death. Light things, such as chaff and feathers, are quickly blown away, but a tree that is rooted survives the storm. He who is rooted in love, endures. True love never ends.

Thomas Watson

LOVE AND THE FAITHFUL FATHER—MAY 17

Know therefore that the LORD your God is God. Deuteronomy 7:9 NRSV

What is obedience? It is doing God's will. It is keeping His commandments. Does God give commandments that we cannot obey? Is He so arbitrary, so severe, and so unloving as to issue commandments that cannot be obeyed? The answer is that in all of holy scripture not a single instance is recorded of God having commanded any person to do a thing that was beyond that person's power. Is God so inconsiderate as to require of us that which we are unable to render? Surely not.

Let us ponder this thought a moment: Do earthly parents require of their children duties that they cannot perform? Where is the father who would think of being so unjust and so tyrannical? Is God less kind and less just than faulty, earthly parents? Are they better and more just than a perfect God? How utterly foolish and untenable a thought!

Edward McKendree Bounds

May 18—Linger in the Gallery of Love

I will make with you an everlasting covenant, my steadfast, sure love for David.
Isaiah 55:3 NRSV

Seek feeling and you will miss it. Be content to live without it, and you will have all you require. If you are always noticing your heartbeats, you will bring on heart disease. If you are ever muffling against cold, you will become very subject to chills. If you are perpetually thinking about your health, you will induce disease. If you are always consulting your feelings, you will live in a dry and thirsty land.

Be indifferent to emotion. If it is there, be thankful. If it is absent, go on doing the will of God, counting on Him, and speaking well of Him. It is impossible to rush into God's presence, catch up anything we fancy, and run off with it. To attempt this will end in mere delusion and disappointment. Nature will not unveil her rarest beauty to the chance tourist. Pictures that are the result of a life of work do not disclose their secret loveliness to those who stroll down a gallery. And God's best cannot be ours apart from patient waiting in His holy presence.

Get into the presence of Jesus, and you will be told clearly and unmistakably His will.

F. B. Meyer

May 19—Love Like Christ

For the love of Christ urges us on, because we are convinced that one has died for all;
therefore all have died. 2 Corinthians 5:14 NRSV

If our Father permits a trial to come, it must be because that trial is the best thing that could happen to us. We must accept it with thanks from His hand. The trial may be hard upon us, and I do not mean that we can enjoy the suffering of it. But we can and must love the will of God in the trial because His will is always sweet, whether it be in joy or in sorrow.

If you are really one with Christ, you will be sweet to those who are cross to you. You will bear everything and make no complaints. When you are reviled, you will not revile again and feel nothing but love in return. You will seek the honor of others rather than your own. You will take the lowest place and be the servant of all, as Christ was. You will literally and truly love your enemies and do good to them who despitefully use you. You will, in short, live a Christlike life and show outwardly—as well as feel inwardly—a Christlike spirit. This is what it is to be one with Christ.

Hannah Whitall Smith

[Love] is not easily provoked. 1 Corinthians 13:5 KJV

*G*ood temper is a remarkable ingredient in love. We are inclined to look upon bad temper as a very harmless weakness. We speak of it as a mere infirmity of nature, a family failing, a matter of temperament, not a thing to take into very serious account in estimating a person's character. And yet right in the heart of Paul's analysis of love in 1 Corinthians 13:5, it finds a place: Love is not easily provoked.

The truth is there are two great classes of sins—sins of the body and sins of the disposition. The prodigal son may be taken as a type of the first, his elder brother of the second. Now society has no doubt whatever as to which of these is the worse. Its brand falls, without a challenge, upon the prodigal. But are we right? We have no balance to weigh one another's sins, and coarser and finer are but human words; faults in the higher nature may be less excusable than those in the lower, and to the eye of Him who is love, a sin against love may seem a hundred times more dishonorable.

Henry Drummond

SINGULAR LOVE—MAY 21

But I will sing of your strength, in the morning I will sing of your love;
for you are my fortress, my refuge in times of trouble. Psalm 59:16 NIV

*W*ith singular love, the soul is Jesus loving, Jesus thinking, and Jesus desiring. It is burning in longing only for Him, singing in Him, resting on Him. Then the thought turns to song and melody. The soul that is in this degree may boldly say, "I mourn for love! I languish to come to my loved Jesus."

He who most withdraws his love from the world and from unreasonable lusts shall be most able and shall most speedily increase in love. Those who have a liking to things other than Jesus and in the sweetness of His law do not come to singular love. He who has singular love desires to be unbound from the bond of his body and to be in full joy with Jesus, whom he loves. In this manner shall a lover of Jesus Christ be. He shall so burn in love that he shall be wholly turned into the fire of love.

John Wycliffe

For I am not ashamed of the gospel. Romans 1:16 NRSV

I will present these things as helps to the knowledge of the nature of the love of Christ and helps to retain it. First, you cannot know the love of Christ before you know the badness of your nature. He who sees but little of his sinful nature will hardly know much of the love of Christ. He who sees of himself nothing at all will hardly ever see anything of the love of Christ. But he who sees most of what a miserable character he is, he is likely to see most of what is the love of Christ. So then if a man would be kept sure and steadfast, let him labor before all things to know his own wretchedness.

Labor to see the emptiness, shortness, and pollution that clings to a man's own righteousness. This also must in some measure be known before a man can know the nature of the love of Christ.

To know the nature of Christ's love, be much in acquainting yourself with the nature of the law and the nature of the gospel. The law is a servant, both first and last, to the gospel. For there is nothing that Satan more desires than that the law may take the place of Christ and faith.

John Bunyan

MAY 23—LOVE AND THE NEW COVENANT

"O LORD, God of Israel, there is no God like you in heaven above or on earth beneath."
1 Kings 8:23 NRSV

I f anyone thinks he believes in Christ and has not the law written in his heart to love his brother as Christ loved him, the faith of that person is vain. It is built upon sand of his own imagination and not upon the rock of God's Word. True faith makes a man to love his brother.

Our service to Christ is only to believe in Him for the remission of sin, to call upon Him and give Him thanks, and to love our neighbors for His sake. Now they who believe in Christ for the remission of their sins and for His sake love their foes are not Christ's enemies. Sin is forgiven only for Christ's sake; and again, our duty is to love our neighbors no less than Christ loved us. Let us exhort each other to trust in Christ and to love each other as Christ did.

William Tyndale

This is how we can be sure that we are in union with him. 1 John 2:5 ISV

There are many relations in life that require from the different parties only very moderate degrees of devotion. We may have pleasant friendships with one another and yet spend a large part of our lives in separate interests and widely differing pursuits. There is not enough love between us to give us the desire to share one another's most private affairs.

But there are other relations in life where all this is changed. The friendship becomes love. The two hearts give themselves to one another. A union of souls takes place, which makes all that belong to one the property of the other. Separate interests and separate paths in life are no longer possible. The reserve and distance suitable to mere friendship gives way to love. The wishes of one become binding obligations to the other. The deepest desire of each heart is that it may know every secret wish or longing of the other so that it may fly on the wings of the wind to gratify it.

Do such as these chafe under this yoke which love imposes? Do they envy the cool, calm, reasonable friendships they see around them, and regret the nearness into which their souls are brought to their beloved one because of the obligations it creates? No, they glory in these very obligations. All the tender, longing love of your heavenly Master makes love a blessing and longed-for privilege.

Hannah Whitall Smith

THE HOLY SPIRIT'S LOVE—MAY 25

For we know how dearly God loves us, because he has given us the Holy Spirit to fill our hearts with his love. Romans 5:5 NLT

It is very important to have clear thoughts about the third Person of the Trinity. Many Christians fail in this respect, and lose much in consequence. He has as distinct a personality as the Son of God. We must not think or speak of Him vaguely, as though He were an influence merely and not a Person. Our Savior teaches us that we should know Him, "for He abideth with you, and shall be in you."

It is the purpose of God that the presence and the love of the Spirit should be made known to those in whom He dwells. Many a believer to whom Christ has left peace knows little of it, but those who are filled with the Spirit are filled with peace. The fruit of the Spirit is love, joy, peace.

Hudson Taylor

MAY 26—JOY AND HAPPINESS

*Satisfy us in the morning with your unfailing love, that we may
sing for joy and be glad all our days. Psalm 90:14 NIV*

*I*f anyone asks the question, "How can I be a happy Christian?" our
Lord's answer is very simple: "I have spoken to you, that My joy may be in
you, and that your joy may be fulfilled." To many Christians, the thought
of a life wholly dwelling in Christ is one of strain and painful effort. They
cannot see that the strain and effort only come when we do not yield ourselves unreservedly to the life of Christ in us.

We are to have Christ's own joy in us. And what is Christ's own joy?
There is no joy like love. There is no joy but love. Christ had spoken of
the Father's love and His own residing in joy, and of His having loved us
with that same love. His joy is nothing but the joy of love, of being loved
and of loving. He wants us to share the joy of being loved of the Father
by our loving and living for those around us. This is just the joy of being
truly branches—living in His love and then giving up ourselves in love to
bear fruit for others.

Andrew Murray

MAY 27—DEVOTED TO MISSIONARY WORK

*We ought always to thank God for you, brothers, and rightly so, because your faith
is growing more and more, and the love every one of you has for each other
is increasing. 2 Thessalonians 1:3 NIV*

*W*e have sent out missionaries with a bare subsistence only and are un-
sparing in our applause of some for not being worldly minded whom our
stinginess made to live as did the prodigal son. I do not speak of myself,
nor need I to do so, but for that very reason I feel at liberty to interpose a
word in behalf of others.

The command to "go into all the world and preach the gospel to every creature" must be obeyed by Christians either personally or by substi-
tute. Now it is quite possible to find people whose love for the heathen
and devotion to the work will make them ready to go forth on the terms
"bare subsistence." But what can be thought of the justice of Christians
and churches who not only work their substitutes at the lowest terms but
regard what they give as charity! The matter is the more grave in respect to
the missionary who may have a wife and family.

David Livingstone

Act on the principles of love and justice, and always live in
confident dependence on your God. Hosea 12:6 NLT

 ove performs the most onerous duties with all its heart if they advance the comfort and help of those whom it loves more than itself. A mother or wife performs tasks from which the hired person would shrink. She does them with all her heart, not considering for a moment the disagreeableness and hardness of the demand. So if we look at our lifework as appointed by God, if we can hear the voice of Jesus saying, "Do this for Me," there is no further thought of hardship or distaste. Remember to do all your lifework for Jesus. Do all in His name and for His glory. Ask Him to fill your heart with submissive, loyal obedience. You will find that when you introduce the personal element of service to Christ into the most ordinary acts, they will glisten like a piece of gold tapestry.

F. B. Meyer

Love, Envy, and Kindness—May 29

Love is not envious or boastful or arrogant. 1 Corinthians 13:4 NRSV

 ove does not envy. This indeed is implied when it is said, "Love is kind." For kindness and envy are inconsistent: They can no more reside together than light and darkness. If we earnestly desire happiness to all, we cannot be grieved at the happiness of any. The fulfilling of our desire will be sweet to our soul. So we will not be pained at their happiness. If we are always doing what good we can for our neighbor and wishing we could do more, it is impossible that we should brood at a good he receives. Instead it will be the very joy of our heart. No matter how we may flatter ourselves or one another, he who envies has not love.

It follows that love is not rash or hasty in judging. As many as love their neighbor for God's sake will not easily listen to an ill opinion of anyone to whom they wish all good, spiritual as well as secular. They cannot condemn him even in their heart without evidence nor upon slight evidence. Indeed, upon any evidence, if it is possible, have him and his accuser brought face-to-face. Or, at the least, inform him of the accusation and let him speak for himself. Every one of you feels that he cannot but act like this with regard to one whom he tenderly loves. He who does not act this way has not love.

John Wesley

Many are the woes of the wicked, but the LORD's unfailing love
surrounds the man who trusts in him. Psalm 32:10 NIV

*D*ear Mr. Partridge,

Nearly every time the newspapers come that you send, I feel so ashamed of my not having written sooner. What a world of unrest, doubt, and pessimism you seem to live in at home. There seems to be no solid foundation for mankind to rest on. Does it point to our Lord's near approach in the Second Coming? I think so, and I hope so! My only drawback is that I fear my children [twins and other children who were abandoned and outcast by natives at Calabar, West Africa] are not all ready. But they are His, and He surely has infinitely more interest and love in and for them than I have, so He will do all things well for us all. He will not throw back the children given to Him in loving trust.

I have had a rebuke this morning from 1 John 4:18, the last clause: "He that feareth is not made perfect in love." How dishonoring to our Father to keep misunderstanding Him and imputing anything unworthy to Him.

Things here go on smoothly. We thank God for a willing people and for the adherence of the young. It is a hard fight with heathenism. They all want their children educated, but they don't want them to serve Christ. Whenever the Christian and heathen practices clash, they are fiercely on the heathen side. Few of the women are moving Christward, although they are friendly and kind to us personally.

Mary Slessor

He defends the cause of the fatherless and the widow, and loves the
alien, giving him food and clothing. Deuteronomy 10:18 NIV

believe that Christ's yoke is easy. And I believe it is an easier way than any other. I believe it is a happier way than any other. The most obvious lesson in Christ's teaching is that there is no happiness in having and getting anything, but only in giving. And half the world is on the wrong scent in the pursuit of happiness. They think it consists in having and getting, and in being served by others. It consists in giving and in serving others. He who would be great among you, said Christ, let him serve. He who would be happy, let him remember that there is but one way—it is more blessed, it is more happy to give than to receive.

Henry Drummond

Two Labor in Love—June 1

For God is not unjust to forget your work and labor of love
which you have shown toward His name. Hebrews 6:10 NKJV

consider it one of the special mercies that this day I have as much desire as ever, yes, more than ever, to live for Him who has done so much for me. My greatest grief is that I love Him so little. I desire many things concerning myself, but I desire nothing so much as to have a heart filled with love to the Lord. I long for a warm, personal attachment to Him.

I consider it further an exceedingly great mercy that I have been kept in uninterrupted love and union with my brother, friend, and fellow-laborer Henry Craik. Very few of the blessings that the Lord has bestowed on him, on me, and on the two churches, whose servants we are, are of greater importance. There is not one point of importance as it regards the truth on which we differ. In judgment as to matters connected with the welfare of the saints among whom we labor, we have been almost invariably at once of one mind.

We have had much joy on account of the scriptural conduct of many of the children of God among whom we labor. The two churches have shown, in some measure, that even in our day there can be love among the brethren. We have had much more joy than sorrow during the last five years.

George Müller

But I say unto you which hear, Love your enemies, do good to them which hate you.
Luke 6:27 KJV

*I*t is a smaller thing to wish well or even to do well to one who has done you no evil. It is far greater—a sort of magnificent goodness—to love your enemy and always to wish him well, and do well to him who wishes you ill and who does you harm when he can.

If one seeks forgiveness, he should no longer be regarded as an enemy, and it should not now be as difficult to love him as it was when he was actively hostile. Now a man who does not forgive from the heart one who asks forgiveness and is repentant of his sins can in no way suppose that his own sins are forgiven by the Lord. The One who, when He was teaching the prayer, strongly emphasized this sentence, saying: "For if you forgive men their trespasses, your heavenly Father will also forgive your trespasses. But if you will not forgive men, neither will your Father forgive your offenses."

Augustine

JUNE 3—LOVE AND TENDERNESS

He ransoms me from death and surrounds me with love and tender mercies.
Psalm 103:4 NLT

*D*iscomfort and unrest are impossible to the souls who come to know that God is their real and actual Father. I must make it plain that it is a father, such as our highest instincts tell us a good father ought to be, of whom I am speaking. Sometimes earthly fathers are unkind or tyrannical or selfish or even cruel—or they are merely indifferent and neglectful—but none of these can be called good fathers. But God, who is good, must be a good father or not a father at all. We must all of us have known good fathers in this world or at least can imagine them. I knew one, and he filled my childhood with sunshine by his most lovely fatherhood. I have learned to know a little about the perfect fatherhood of God because of my experience with this lovely earthly father.

We must heap together all the best of all the fathers and mothers we have ever known or can imagine, and we must tell ourselves that this is only a faint image of God, our Father in heaven. What a good father ought to do, God, who is our Father, is absolutely sure to do.

Hannah Whitall Smith

These were more noble than those in Thessalonica, in that they received the
word with all readiness of mind, and searched the scriptures daily,
whether those things were so. Acts 17:11 KJV

Love is an excellent thing, a very great blessing indeed. It makes every difficulty easy and bears all wrongs with composure. For it bears a burden without being weighted and renders sweet all that is bitter. The noble love of Jesus spurs to great deeds and excites longing for that which is more perfect. Love tends upward; it will not be held down by anything low. Love wishes to be free and estranged from all worldly affections lest its inward sight be obstructed, lest it be entangled in any transitory interest and overcome by adversity.

Nothing is sweeter than love, nothing stronger or higher or wider; nothing is more pleasant, nothing fuller, and nothing better in heaven or on earth, for love is born of God and cannot rest except in God who is above all created things.

Thomas à Kempis

Forsaken Love—June 5

Can a woman forget her nursing child. . . ? Isaiah 49:15 NRSV

Love of your children should move you to serve the Lord. Most people express a great fondness for their children. Very often their own lives are wrapped up in those of their offspring. "Can a woman forget her sucking child?" asks God by His prophet Isaiah. He speaks of it as a monstrous thing and scarcely credible, but the words immediately following affirm it to be possible: "Yes, they may forget." Experience also assures us they may. Father and mother may both forsake their children, for what greater degree of forgetfulness can they express toward them than to neglect bringing them up in the knowledge and fear of God?

How can it be expected they should learn their duty, except those set over them take care to teach it to them? The more they are taught their duty to God, the better they will perform their duties to you. To neglect the improvement of their souls, out of a dread of spending too much time in religious duties, is acting quite contrary to your own interest as well as duty.

George Whitefield

JUNE 6—CRY FOR HELP

Above all, love each other deeply, because love covers over a multitude of sins. 1 Peter 4:8 NIV

*T*hose who will turn truly to Christ must flee situations, sights, and deeds that tempt them to sin. He who is truly fed with the bread that came down from heaven bows not his love to those things to which the evil one entices. Temptations are overcome by patience and meek suffering. What is patience? It is a glad and willing suffering of troubles. He who is patient murmurs not at adversity, but rather at all times praises God.

He who truly loves his Maker refuses to desire any things that are in the world. It is sweetness for him to speak of Him and be with Him. To think upon his Maker is refreshing to him. The fiery darts of the enemy are put out with the meekness and sweetness of the love of Christ. Therefore, when we are tempted, let us cry for the help of our Father, as a child cries after the comfort of its mother.

John Wycliffe

JUNE 7—LOVE TO TEACH CHILDREN

He will bless the babies from your womb. Deuteronomy 7:13 TM

I found a teacher at our services when she ought to have been attending to her class. Upon my asking why she was at our meeting, she said: "I have a very small class—only five little boys."

"What?" said I. "You have come here and neglected these little ones! Why, in that little head may be the seeds of a reformation. There may be a Luther, a Wheaton, a Wesley, or a Bunyan among them. You may be neglecting a chance for them, the effects of which will follow them through life."

Look what a kind teacher did in southern Illinois. She had taught a little girl to love the Savior, and the teacher asked her, "Can you get your father to come to Sunday school?" This father was a swearing, drinking man, and the love of God was not in his heart. But under the training of that teacher, the little girl went to her father, told him of Jesus' love, and led him to that Sunday school. What was the result? I heard before leaving for Europe that her father had been instrumental in founding over 780 Sunday schools in southern Illinois.

What a privilege a teacher has—a privilege of leading souls to Christ. Let every Sunday school teacher say, "By the help of God I will try to lead my scholars to Christ."

Dwight Lyman Moody

This is how God showed his love among us: He sent his one and only
Son into the world that we might live through him. 1 John 4:9 NIV

*I*t may be reasonably asked, "If God so loved the world with a love characterized by only greatness, why did He not save all the world without sacrificing His Son?" This question suffices to show us that there is deep meaning in this word. It was not a mere emotion or feeling. It was not a blind impulse. God had emotion but not emotion only. Indeed the Bible everywhere teaches us that God's love for man, lost in his sins, was paternal—the love of a father for his offspring—in this case, for a rebellious, disobedient, prodigal offspring. In this love there must of course blend the deepest compassion.

Charles Finney

INCREASE IN LOVE—JUNE 9

. . .the LORD, a God merciful and gracious, slow to anger. . . Exodus 34:6–7 NRSV

*E*very act of love to a sin is a perfect enemy to the love of God. It is a great shame to take any part of our affection from the eternal God and bestow it upon his creature in defiance of the Creator. Remove worldly cares and multitudes of secular businesses because if these take up the intention and actual application of our thoughts, they will also possess our passions. If we dwell in the affairs of the world, we shall also grow in love with them, and all our love shall be spent upon trifles and vanities.

Talk with God by frequent prayer. In particular, ask that your desires may be right—and love to have your affections with Him regular and holy. Call to Him for health, run to Him for counsel, and beg of Him for pardon. It is as natural to love Him to whom we make such addresses and on whom we have such dependencies as it is for children to love their parents. For it is not my governor, my employer, or my friend who supports me or provides my needs, but God.

Jeremy Taylor

JUNE 10—COPY GOD'S LOVE

*"He who loves me will be loved by my Father, and I too will
love him and show myself to him." John 14:21 NIV*

*F*orgiving our enemies is hard. We are apt to forget kindnesses and remember injuries, but if we love God, we shall leave behind offences. When
we seriously consider how many affronts and provocations He has put up
with at our hands, this makes us copy Him and endeavor to bury an injury
than to retaliate it.

Love made Christ suffer for us. Love was the chain that fastened
Him to the cross. If we love God, we shall be willing to suffer for Him.
Love is the most suffering grace. It will suffer reproaches, bonds, and im-
prisonments for Christ's sake. Love will carry men out above their own
strength. How did divine affection carry the early saints above the love of
life and the fear of death! These divine heroes were willing to suffer rather
than by their cowardice to make the name of God suffer. They refused to
come out of prison on sinful terms.

Many will not forego the least comfort or undergo the least cross for
His sake. May not Christ suspect us when we pretend to love Him and yet
will endure nothing for Him?

Thomas Watson

JUNE 11—LOVE ONE ANOTHER

"My command is this: Love each other as I have loved you." John 15:12 NIV

*N*othing can be more natural than that Christians should love one
another, even as Christ loved them. The life they received from their
heavenly vine is nothing but love. This is the one thing He asks above all
others: "Hereby shall all men know that you are My disciples: Love one
another." As the special sort of vine is known by the fruit it bears, the nature of the heavenly vine is to be judged by the love His disciples have to
one another.

Love your fellow Christians as the way to stay in the love of your Lord.
Let your interaction with the Christians in your own family be holy, tender,
Christlike love. Let your thoughts of the Christians around you be in the
spirit of Christ's love. Let your life and conduct be the sacrifice of love—
give yourself up to think of their needs to help and to serve them. The life
Christ lives in you is love. As you live out your life, let it be all love.

Andrew Murray

May our LORD Jesus Christ himself. . .encourage your hearts
and strengthen you. 2 Thessalonians 2:16–17 NIV

With a former theology, man as man as a human being was of no account. He was a mere theological unit, an unknown quantity. He was taught to believe, therefore not to love. Now we are learning slowly that to believe is to love: that the first commandment is to love God, and the second like unto it—another version of it—is to love man. Not only the happiness but also the efficiency of love as a power and as a practical success in the world is coming to be recognized.

The fact that Christ led no army, He wrote no book, spent no money, but that He loved and so conquered, this is beginning to strike men. And Paul's argument is gaining adherents that when all prophecies are fulfilled, and all our knowledge becomes obsolete, and all tongues grow unintelligible, this thing, love, will abide and see them all out one by one into the oblivious past. This is the hope for the world: that we shall learn to love, and in learning that, unlearn all anger and wrath and evil speaking and malice and bitterness.

Henry Drummond

LOVE EVERLASTING—JUNE 13

But the steadfast love of the LORD is from everlasting to everlasting. . . . Psalm 103:17 NRSV

Mothers do not let their children forget them. If the boy has gone to Australia and does not write home, his mother writes, "Has John forgotten his mother?" Then there comes back a sweet letter. So is it with Jesus. He says, "Remember Me." Our response is, "We will remember Your love."

Your love is ancient as the glory that You had with the Father before the world was. We remember Your eternal love when You embraced us. We remember the love that suggested the sacrifice of Yourself. We remember Your love as it was manifest to us in Your holy life, from the manger of Bethlehem to the garden of Gethsemane. We track You from the cradle to the grave—for every word and deed of Yours was love. We rejoice in Your love that death did not exhaust Your love that shone resplendent in Your resurrection. We remember that burning fire of love that will never let You hold Your peace until Your chosen ones are all safely housed, until Zion is glorified, and Jerusalem settled on her everlasting foundations of light and love in heaven.

Charles Haddon Spurgeon

JUNE 14—LOVE AS AN EMOTION

Your love has given me great joy and encouragement, because you, brother, have refreshed the hearts of the saints. Philemon 7 NIV

*T*he most spiritual person may at times be without any consciousness of this sensibility and of the joy which accompanies it. At other times he may realize a love divine burning in his heart like a furnace glowing with seven-fold intensity. These spiritual phenomena do not seem to be regulated by any law other than this: that they occur only in those who have the most intimate knowledge of Christ and are the most surrendered to His will.

The purpose of love as a feeling is to awaken joy and not only to cheer and encourage the believer amid his conflicts, but also to strengthen love as a principle, which is absolutely essential to Christian character. Christian love as a principle seems to be a composite embracing an intellectual agreement to the truth of Christ's claims, an admiration of the stainless purity of His character, and an irreversible self-surrender of the will to His authority as a sovereign, to His infallibility as a teacher, and to His sufficiency as the only Savior from the guilt of sin and the love of sin.

Daniel Steele

JUNE 15—THE LOVING HEART

So now, O Israel, what does the LORD your God require of you? Deuteronomy 10:12 NRSV

*W*e naturally credit right motives to those whom we love, and put the best allowable interpretation upon their words and deeds. A lack of this is evidence conclusive of an unloving heart in regard to professed converts. Charity, or love, is very ready to judge kindly and favorably of those who profess to be converted to Christ, and will naturally watch over them with interest, pray for them, instruct them, and have as much confidence in them as it is reasonable to have.

We always enjoy the saying and doing of those things that please those whom we most love. If we do not enjoy the service of God, it is because we do not truly serve Him. If we love Him supremely, it is impossible that we should not enjoy His service at every step. Always remember that whenever you lose your enjoyment of serving God, you may know that you are not serving Him right.

While the heart is full of the love of God, God is feared and not man. A desire for the applause of men is kept down, and it is enough to please God, whether men are pleased or displeased.

Charles Finney

For the love of God is this, that we obey his commandments.
And his commandments are not burdensome.
1 John 5:3 NRSV

I never knew anyone to come to Christ yet who did not have to give up something. But the only things God asks you to give up are the things that are doing you harm. God has given to each one of us a guarantee that He will never ask us to give up anything that is for our good, and that guarantee is His own Son. I do not think if God has given His Son to die for us, He is going to ask us to give up anything that is good for us.

I remember when once I was talking to a young lady about coming to Christ. She said, "Well, I would like to be a Christian. But there is too much to give up."

I said, "Do you think God loves you?"

"I know He does," she replied.

"How much do you think God loves you?"

"God loved me enough to give His Son to die for me," she said.

I said, "Do you think that God, if He loved you enough to give His Son to die for you, will ask you to give up anything that is good for you to keep?"

She said, "No, He will not."

I said, "Do you want to keep anything that is not for your highest good?"

She replied, "No."

"Then do you not think you would better come to Christ right now?"

She said, "I will," and she did.

Reuben Archer Torrey

"How often I have longed to gather your children together, as a hen gathers her chicks under her wings, but you were not willing!" Luke 13:34 NIV

God combines both father and mother in one, in our highest ideals of both. He comprises all the love, tenderness, and self-sacrifice that we cannot but recognize to be the essence of parenting. Although we know perfectly well that He says He does care for us in just this tender and loving way, yet we say, "If I could only believe that, of course I should be comforted." Now here is just where our wills must come in. We must believe it. We must say to ourselves, "God says it, and it is true, and I am going to believe it no matter how it looks." Then we must never suffer ourselves to doubt or question it again.

My own experience as a child taught me this beyond any possibility of question. My mother was the remedy for all my own ills and, I fully believed, for the ills of the whole world, if only they could be brought to her. When anyone expressed doubts as to her capacity to remedy everything, I remembered with what fine scorn I used to annihilate them by saying, "Ah, but you don't know my mother!"

Hannah Whitall Smith

JUNE 18—HEART FULL OF LOVE

"...to love the LORD your God, to walk in all his ways, to obey his commands, to hold fast to him and to serve him with all your heart and all your soul." Joshua 22:5 NIV

There is," remarks one of the old Puritans, "a straitness, slavery, and narrowness in all sin. Sin crumples up our souls, which if they were freely spread abroad would be as large and wide as the whole universe. Any man who has his will enlarged to the extent of God's will, by loving whatever God loves and nothing else, enjoys boundless liberty and a boundless sweetness."

God's love embraces the universe. We who have partaken of the divine nature must also love as He does. Thomas à Kempis says, "He who desires glory in things outside of God, or to take pleasure in some private good, shall many ways be encumbered and confined. But if heavenly grace enters in and true charity, there will be no envy or narrowness of heart; neither will self-love busy itself because divine charity overcomes all things and enlarges all the powers of the soul." Give unto us, God, this largeness of heart!

F. B. Meyer

The amazing grace of the Master, Jesus Christ, the extravagant love of God, the intimate friendship of the Holy Spirit, be with all of you. 2 Corinthians 13:14 TM

*H*ow do you and I wish we had known Jesus sooner, and that we had more of His love? It is amazing love; it is forgiving love; it is dying love; it is exalted and interceding love; and it is glorified love. I am talking of the love of Jesus Christ who loved me before I loved Him. He saw me polluted in blood, full of sores, a slave to sin, death, and hell, running to destruction. Then He said unto my soul, "Live." He snatched me as a brand plucked from the burning. It was love that saved me. It was all of the free grace of God and that only.

If there are any here who are strangers to this love of the Lord Jesus Christ, do not despair. Come, come unto Christ, and He will have mercy upon you. He will pardon all your sins. He will love you freely and take you to be with Himself. You need not fear, you need not despair when God has had mercy upon such a wretch as I. And He will save you also if you will come unto Him by faith.

George Whitefield

LOVE AND COURTESY—JUNE 20

[Love] doth not behave itself unseemly. 1 Corinthians 13:5 KJV

*C*ourtesy is love in society. It is love in relation to etiquette. Politeness has been defined as love in trifles. Courtesy is said to be love in little things. And the one secret of politeness is to love. Love cannot behave itself unseemly. You can put the most untutored persons into the highest society, and if they have a reservoir of love in their hearts, they will not behave themselves unseemly. They simply cannot do it.

You know the meaning of the word *gentleman*. It means a gentle man—a man who does things gently and with love. And that is the whole art and mystery of it. The gentleman cannot in the nature of things do an ungentle, an ungentlemanly thing. The ungentle soul, the inconsiderate, unsympathetic nature cannot do anything else.

People are devoted, and rightly, to their rights. But there come times when people may exercise even the higher right of giving up their rights. Love strikes much deeper. It would have us not seek them at all, ignore them, and eliminate the personal element altogether from our calculations. It is not hard to give up our rights. They are often external.

Henry Drummond

June 21—Love in the Heart

"For man looks at the outward appearance, but the LORD looks at the heart."
1 Samuel 16:7 *NKJV*

Ask yourself whether you have ever in your lives brought forth any fruit to God. Have you ever done anything from a gracious respect to God or out of love to God? By only seeking your worldly interest, you do not bring forth fruit to God. To be sober, moral, and religious only to be seen of men or out of respect to your own credit and honor does not bring forth fruit to God. How is doing that for God, which is only for the sake of custom or to be esteemed of men?

There is no fruit brought forth to God where there is nothing done from love to God or from any true respect to Him. God looks at the heart. He does not stand in need of our services, neither is He benefited by anything that we can do. He does not receive anything of us because it benefits Him, but only as a suitable testimony of our love and respect to Him. This is the fruit that He seeks.

Jonathan Edwards

June 22—Colored with Love

My child, keep your father's commandment, and do not forsake your mother's teaching.
Proverbs 6:20 *NRSV*

A man sent a friend of mine some crystals from the Scientific American and said: "One of these crystals as small as a pinpoint will give a noticeable green hue to 7,000 gallons of water." Think of it! Power enough in an atom to color 7,000 gallons of water. There is power in a word or act to adversely influence a boy and through him afflict a community. There is power enough in a word to color the life of that child so it will become a power to lift the world to Jesus Christ. The mother will put in motion influences that will either touch heaven or hell. Talk about greatness!

There is power in a mother's love. A mother's love must be like God's love. How God could ever tell the world that He loved it without a mother's example has often puzzled me. If the devils in hell ever turned pale, it was the day mother's love flamed up for the first time in a woman's heart.

Billy Sunday

For the LORD is good; his mercy is everlasting; and his truth endureth to all generations.
Psalm 100:5 KJV

*L*ove in Christ does not lean toward undue or unlawful objects. It always acts according to God, and at anytime there is not the least shadow of swerving. Love in Christ requires no beauty in the object to be beloved. Because we fully do not know love, He comes down to our capacities and speaks about His love to us according as we find love to work in ourselves. He describes His love by borrowing from us instances of our love to wife and children.

Love in Christ decays not. It cannot be tempted to do so by anything that happens. This love continues to act until all things that are imperfections are completely and everlastingly subdued. The reason is that Christ loves to make us pleasing and wholesome, not because we are so.

John Bunyan

MEASURING LOVE—JUNE 24

Whom have I in heaven but you? And there is nothing on earth
that I desire other than you. Psalm 73:25 NRSV

*I*f the world were placed in one scale and Christ in the other, He must weigh heaviest. If one had a friend who supplied him continually with money and gave him all his allowance, were not he worse than a barbarian who did not respect and honor that friend? Such a friend is God. He gives you breath, and He bestows a livelihood upon you. Will you not love Him?

When the body is cold and has no heat, it is a sign of death. That man is dead who has no heat of love in his soul to God. This reproof falls heavy upon the infidels of this age who are so far from loving God that they do all they can to show their hatred of Him. Oh, how far are they from being lovers of God, who scarcely ever think of God! A sinner crowds God out of his thoughts. He never thinks of God unless with horror, as the prisoner thinks of the judge.

Thomas Watson

The earth, O LORD, is full of your steadfast love; teach me your statutes. Psalm 119:64 NRSV

The master of one of the schools in Bristol reports: "I am thankful to say that there is a spirit of inquiry among the boys, and I hope one or two have accepted the Lord Jesus as their Savior."

Another teacher reports: "I feel thankful that I have again the privilege of bearing testimony to the goodness and mercy of God through the past year. My heart has been greatly cheered and encouraged by seeing the work of the Holy Spirit among my dear scholars. From personal conversation with them, I found several were earnestly seeking Jesus. One dear girl was rejoicing that He loved her. Another little girl wrote me a little letter in which she expressed her hope that God would bless her. She also added, 'I would like to love Jesus with my whole heart because I know He loves me and has died to save me.' Another dear child was melted to tears by the simple story of Christ's love.

"The earnest attention which the dear children give to the Word of God is also a cause of much thankfulness. Many have given evidence that they have been impressed by the truth of God. There is an eagerness amongst the children to know the truth of God."

The child of God should make it his particular business to encourage sinners to seek after the Lord, and to increase the faith and love of the brethren through speaking well of the name of the Lord.

George Müller

JUNE 26—LOVE FOR THE CHURCH

No one hates his own body but lovingly cares for it, just as Christ cares for his body, which is the church. Ephesians 5:29 NLT

History shows that whenever God uses a rod to chasten His servants, He always breaks it afterward as if He loathed the rod that gave His children pain. Like a father pities his children, so the Lord pities them who fear Him.

If this is true of His church collectively, it is also true of each individual member. You may fear that the Lord has passed you by, but it is not so. He who counts the stars and calls them by their names is in no danger of forgetting His own children. He knows your case as thoroughly as if you were the only creature He ever made or the only saint He ever loved. Approach Him and be at peace.

Charles Haddon Spurgeon

*Has not God chosen those who are poor in the eyes of the world to be rich in faith
and to inherit the kingdom he promised those who love him? James 2:5 NIV*

We may lose heart and hope, our head may turn dizzy, our heart faint, and the mocking voices of our foes suggest that God has forgotten or forsaken us. But He remains faithful. He cannot deny Himself. He cannot throw aside responsibilities that He has assumed. Often I have gone to God in desperate need, aggravated by nervous depression and heart sickness, and said, "My faith is flickering out. Its hand seems paralyzed, its eye blinded, its old glad song silenced forever. But You are faithful, and I am counting on You!"

The soul loves to stand upon the promises of God. We find no difficulty in trusting our friends because we open our hearts, like south windows, to their love. Where would be our difficulty about faith if we ceased worrying about it and were occupied with the object of faith—Jesus Christ our Lord?

F. B. Meyer

BADGE OF LOVE—JUNE 28

"This is my Son, marked by my love, focus of all my delight." 2 Peter 1:17 TM

The Lord Jesus Christ came down from heaven as the Son of God's love. He lived a life of love in fellowship with His disciples, in compassion over the poor and miserable, in love even to His enemies, and He died the death of love. Now Jesus calls us to walk in love. He demands that though a man hate you, still you love him. True love cannot be conquered by anything in heaven or upon the earth. The more hatred there is, the more love triumphs and shows its true nature. This is the love that Christ commanded His disciples to exercise.

You all know what it is to wear a badge. And Christ said to His disciples in effect: "I give you a badge, and that badge is love. That is to be your mark. It is the only thing in heaven or on earth by which men can know Me."

Andrew Murray

June 29—Scene of Love from Paul's Journeys

After saying good-by to each other, we went aboard the ship,
and they returned home. Acts 21:6 NIV

*F*ollowing his visit to Ephesus, Paul arrived at Tyre, where he stopped
a few days. Here he found some disciples who begged Paul not to go to
Jerusalem, saying through the Spirit that he should not go up to that city.
But Paul adhered to his original purpose to go to Jerusalem. The account
says: "But when our time was up, we left and continued on our way. All the
disciples and their wives and children accompanied us out of the city, and
there on the beach we knelt to pray."

What a sight to observe on that seashore! Here is a family picture of
love and devotion, where husbands, wives, and even children are present,
and prayer is made out in the open air. The vessel was ready to depart, but
prayer must cement their affections and bless wives and children, and bless
their parting—a parting which was to be final so far as this world was
concerned. Never did a seashore see a grander picture or witness a lovelier
sight—Paul on his knees on the sands of that shore, invoking God's blessing upon these men, women, and children.

Edward McKendree Bounds

June 30—Love and the Name of Jesus

That we should believe on the name of his son Jesus Christ, and love one another. 1 John 3:23 KJV

*T*he name Jesus, truly held in mind, roots up vices, plants virtues, brings
love to people, gives people a taste of heavenly things, removes discord,
produces peace, gives everlasting rest, and does away with fleshly desires.
It fills those who love it with spiritual joy. The righteous man desires to be
blessed because he has truly loved this name Jesus. He is called righteous
because he seeks earnestly to love Jesus.

The more we love, the more we yearn to love. The love of Jesus by
self is delightful and desirable. Therefore no joy shall be lacking for those
who seek earnestly to love Him whom angels desire to behold. Therefore
many people wish to have joy with Christ, but as they love not His name,
Jesus, they shall have sorrow without end, whatever they do. If they give
all things that they have to poor people, unless they love this name Jesus,
they shall labor in vain.

I sought to love Jesus, and the more I grew complete in His love, so
much the sweeter His Name became to me.

John Wycliffe

Whoever does not love abides in death. 1 John 3:14 NRSV

*O*ne man who died with love called all who were near him by their names and said, "Think of heaven, talk of heaven. All the time is lost when we are not thinking of heaven." Now this was the voice of love.

Another good soldier of Jesus Christ was grappling with his last enemy—death. Some of his last breath was spent in a psalm of praise to Him who was then giving him the victory. He was asked, "Have you the love of God in your heart?" He lifted up his eyes and hands, and answered with the whole strength he had left, "Yes, yes!" To one who asked if he was afraid of the devil, he replied, "No, no. My loving Savior has conquered every enemy: He is with me. I fear nothing." Soon afterward, he fell into a sort of slumber, and his soul sweetly returned to God who gave it.

Perfect love casts out whatever might have caused torment. And whoever you are who has the like measure of love, your end shall be like his.

John Wesley

LOVE ENDURES FOREVER—JULY 2

"Give thanks to the LORD of hosts, for the LORD is good, for his steadfast love endures forever!" Jeremiah 33:11 NRSV

*I*f it is better to love God than the world, surely also it is better to love God than sin. What is there in sin that any should love it? Sin is a debt. Does any man love to be in debt? Sin is a disease. Will any man hug a disease? Will he love his plague sores? Sin is compared to leprosy. Sin is a misshapen monster: Lust makes a man brutish; malice makes him devilish. What is in sin to be loved? It has four stings—shame, guilt, horror, death.

Love is the most abiding grace. This will stay with us when other graces take their farewell. In heaven we shall need no repentance because we shall have no sin. In heaven we shall not need patience because there will be no hardship. In heaven we shall need no faith because faith looks at things unseen. But then we shall see God face-to-face, and where there is vision, there is no need of faith.

But when the other graces are out-of-date, love continues. In this sense love is greater than faith because it abides the longest. Faith is the staff we walk with in this life. But we shall leave this staff at heaven's door, and only love shall enter.

Thomas Watson

*If you really keep the royal law found in Scripture, "Love your
neighbor as yourself," you are doing right. James 2:8 NIV*

We have grace in Christ, that is, promises of life by His merits. In the
gospel, when we believe the promise, we receive the spirit of life. We are
justified in the blood of Christ from all the things that the law condemned
us. And we receive love unto the law, power to fulfill it, and grow in it daily.
Christ brings the love of God unto us.

You see two ways that people are badly deceived. First are those who
justify themselves with outward deeds. They abstain from what the law
forbids and do what the law commands. They set themselves above other
sinners and condemn them. They do not see how the law requires love
from the bottom of their hearts. Those also are deceived who without
all fear of God give themselves unto all manner of vices, having no respect
for the law of God.

By grace we know God as our most merciful Father and consent to
the law, love it, desire to fulfill it, and sorrow because we cannot. But the
blood of Christ has made satisfaction for the rest.

William Tyndale

*You bestow on him blessings forever; you make him glad with the joy of your presence.
Psalm 21:6 NRSV*

Blessing is always accompanied with joy. A little child playing with his
toys may be both happy and satisfied. But the little one hears the mother's footsteps, sees the mother open the door, and instantly the toys are
dropped and forgotten. The little arms are stretched out and the little
feet are running to meet the welcome mother. The motherly arms are as
quickly stretched forth toward the child, and with longer steps the mother
hastens to meet the little one and clasps the child to her bosom.

But whose heart is the more glad? The little one's heart is full. The
mother's heart is also full; but her capacity is greater, and so her joy is
deeper. And is not this true of our heavenly Father? When His heart
blesses ours, and ours blesses Him, we are full of joy. But His heart is infinitely greater than ours, and His joy in His people far exceeds all their joy
in Him as the infinite exceeds the finite.

Hudson Taylor

But just as you excel in everything—in faith, in speech, in knowledge, in complete earnestness and in your love for us—see that you also excel in this grace of giving. 2 Corinthians 8:7 NIV

Zeal must spend its greatest heat principally in those things that concern ourselves, but with great care and restraint in those that concern others. Remember that zeal must in no sense contradict any action of love. Love to God includes love to our neighbor, and therefore no pretence of zeal for God's glory must make us uncharitable to our brother. Doing so is as pleasing to God as hatred is an act of love. Zeal directed to others can spend itself in nothing but charitable actions for their good.

Let loose zeal in matters of internal, personal, and spiritual actions that are matters of direct duty such as prayers and thanksgiving. Zeal is only acceptable and safe when it advances the love of God and our neighbors. In brief, let your zeal (if it must be expressed in anger) be always more severe against yourself than against others.

Jeremy Taylor

MARVELOUS LOVE—JULY 6

So thank GOD for his marvelous love, for his miracle mercy to the children he loves. Psalm 107:21 TM

Marvelous is the only word we can use as we think of the well-beloved Son who descended to the bed in a manger, of the agony and bloody sweat of the cross and passion—and all for us who were His enemies. But it is most marvelous of all that You made us children and joint heirs with Christ. To think that we shall shine as the sun in Your kingdom and be included in that circle of love and life of which the throne of God and the Lamb is the center! Surely the marvels of Your grace will only seem the greater when eternity with its boundless ages gives us time to explore them.

The danger, however, is that we should become strong in our own conceit and credit ourselves with the position which is due to the grace of God alone. We need the truly humble spirit of the little child that we may never boast of ourselves! God cannot trust some of us with prosperity and success because our nature could not stand them.

F. B. Meyer

July 7—I Love the Word of God

"The one who sowed the good seed is the Son of Man." Matthew 13:37 NIV

*I*n the hope that others would be induced to join him in Christianity, Chief Sechele asked me to begin family worship with him in his house. I did so and was surprised to hear how well he conducted the prayer in his own simple and beautiful style, for he was quite a master of his own African language. At this time we were suffering from the effects of a drought, and none except his family, whom he ordered to attend, came near his meeting.

"In former times," said he, "when a chief was fond of hunting, all his people got dogs and became fond of hunting, too. If he was fond of dancing or music, all showed a liking to these amusements, too. If the chief loved beer, they all rejoiced in strong drink. But in this case it is different. I love the Word of God, and not one of my kinsmen will join me."

His friends seemed to think that I [David Livingstone] had thrown a charm over him and that he had become mine. They all treated us still with respectful kindness, but to Sechele himself they said things which, as he often remarked, had they ventured on in former times would have cost them their lives. But we had sown the good seed and have no doubt but it will yet spring up, though we may not live to see the fruits.

David Livingstone

July 8—Love and Happiness

Create in me a clean heart, O God; and renew a right spirit within me. Psalm 51:10 KJV

*A*re you lacking in long-suffering? Then as far as you fall short, you fall short of happiness. The more the opposite tempers—anger, fretfulness, revenge—prevail, the more unhappy you are.

The storm cannot be eased or peace ever returned to your soul unless meekness, gentleness, patience, or, in one word, love, take possession of it. If any man find in himself ill will, malice, envy, or any other temper opposite to kindness, then misery is there. The stronger the temper, the more miserable he is. The soul of the malicious or envious person is the very type of hell—full of torment as well as wickedness. The great gulf is not yet fixed between him and heaven. There is a Spirit still willing to renew his heart in the love of God and so lead him up to eternal happiness.

John Wesley

For their sake he remembered his covenant, and showed compassion according to the abundance of his steadfast love. Psalm 106:45 NRSV

*T*oward whom is this love of God exercised? Toward us—toward all beings of our lost race. To each one of us He manifests this love.

How does He commend this love? By giving His Son to die for us. By giving one who was a Son and a Son well-beloved. It is written that God "gave Him a ransom for all" and that "He tasted death for every man." It is a great mistake into which some fall, to suppose that Christ died for the human race in general and not for each one in particular. By this mistake the gospel is likely to lose much of its practical power on our hearts. So we are to regard Jesus as having loved us personally and individually.

We should think we gave evidence of a strong love if we were to give our friend a great sum of money. But what is any sum of money compared with giving up a dear Son to die? Oh, surely it is surpassing love, beyond measure wonderful, that Jesus should not only labor and suffer but should really die! Was ever love like this?

Charles Finney

Learning Love—July 10

. . . joined and held together by every supporting ligament, grows and builds itself up in love, as each part does its work. Ephesians 4:16 NIV

*I*f a man does not exercise his arm, he develops no biceps muscle; and if a man does not exercise his soul, he acquires no muscle in his soul, no strength of character, no vigor of moral fiber, nor beauty of spiritual growth. Love is a rich, strong, and vigorous expression of the whole round Christian character—the Christlike nature in its fullest development. And the components of this great character are only to be built up by ceaseless practice. What was Christ doing in the carpenter's shop? Practicing. Though perfect, we read that He learned obedience, and He increased in wisdom and in favor with God and man.

Talent develops itself in solitude—the talent of prayer, of faith, of meditation, of seeing the unseen. Character grows in the stream of the world's life. That chiefly is where we are to learn love.

Henry Drummond

Remembering without ceasing your work of faith, and labour of love, and patience of hope in our LORD Jesus Christ, in the sight of God and our Father. 1 Thessalonians 1:3 KJV

What should be believed, what should be hoped for, and what should be loved? You would have the answers to all these questions if you really understood what a man should believe, what he should hope for, and what he ought to love. For these are the chief things to seek for in religion.

You have asked for something you could carry around, not just baggage for your bookshelf. Therefore we may return to these three ways in which, as we said, God should be served: faith, hope, love.

What, then, shall I say of love, without which faith can do nothing? There can be no true hope without love. Indeed, as the apostle James says, "Even the demons believe and tremble." However, they neither hope nor love. Instead, they tremble because they believe as we do that what we hope for is coming to pass. The apostle Paul approves and commends the faith that works by love and that cannot exist without hope. Consequently, it is that love is not without hope, hope is not without love, and neither hope nor love is without faith.

Augustine

JULY 12—LOVE AND JOY

"Rejoice in that day and leap for joy! For indeed your reward is great in heaven." Luke 6:23 NKJV

All Christ's ways of mercy tend to end in the saints' joys. He wept, sorrowed, and suffered that they might rejoice. He sends the Spirit to be our comforter. He multiplies promises and makes known our future happiness that our joy may be full.

Poor, humble, drooping soul, how would it fill you with joy now, if a voice from heaven should tell you of the love of God, the pardon of your sins, and assure you of your part in these heavenly joys? What then will your joy be when your actual possession shall convince you of your title, and you shall be in heaven before you are well aware! It is not your joy only. It is a mutual joy as well as a mutual love. There is joy in heaven at your conversion, and there will be joy at your glorification. The angels will welcome you to heaven and congratulate your safe arrival.

Richard Baxter

For I desire steadfast love and not sacrifice, the knowledge of God rather than burnt offerings.
Hosea 6:6 NRSV

*L*ove is watchful. Sleeping, it does not slumber. Wearied, it is not tired. Pressed, it is not restricted. Alarmed, it is not confused. Love is swift, sincere, kind, pleasant, and delightful. Love is strong, patient and faithful, prudent, and long-suffering. Love is never self-seeking because in whatever a person seeks for himself, there he falls from love. Love is circumspect, humble, and upright. It is not intent upon vain things. It is sober and chaste, firm and quiet, guarded in all the senses.

He who is not ready to suffer all things and to stand resigned to the will of the Beloved is not worthy to be called a lover. A lover must embrace willingly all that is difficult and bitter for the sake of the Beloved, and he should not turn away from Him because of adversities.

Thomas à Kempis

COMPROMISED LOVE—JULY 14

"Quick! Catch all the little foxes before they ruin the vineyard of your love,
for the grapevines are all in blossom." Song of Songs 2:15 NLT

*A*re we not all too apt to seek Him rather because of our need than for His joy and pleasure? This should not be. We do not admire selfish children who only think of what they can get from their parents and are unmindful of the pleasure that they may give or the service that they may render. But are not we in danger of forgetting that pleasing God means giving Him pleasure? Some of us look back to the time when the words "to please God" meant no more than not to sin against Him and not to grieve Him. However, would the love of earthly parents be satisfied with the mere absence of disobedience? Or would a bridegroom be satisfied if his bride only sought him for the supply of her own need?

Ah, how often the enemy succeeds by one device or another in tempting the believer away from that position of entire consecration to Christ in which alone the fullness of His power and of His love can be experienced. Little compromises with the world—disobedience to the still, small voice in little things, little indulgences of the flesh to the neglect of duty—the enemies may be small, but the mischief done is great.

Hudson Taylor

JULY 15—DWELL IN LOVE AND PEACE

My people will live in peaceful dwelling places, in secure homes,
in undisturbed places of rest. Isaiah 32:18 NIV

When we move into a new house, we not only move in ourselves, but we take with us all our belongings, and above all, we take our family. No one would be so foolish as to leave outside anything he cared for or anyone he loved. But I am afraid there are some of God's children who move into the dwelling place of God themselves, but who by their lack of faith leave outside those they love best. More often than not, it is their children who are so abandoned. We would be horrified at a father who in a time of danger should flee into a fortress for safety but should leave his children outside. Yet hundreds of Christians do this very thing. Every anxious thought in which we indulge about our children proves that we have not really taken them with us into the dwelling place of God.

If we trust for ourselves, we must trust for our loved ones, also, and especially for our children. God is more their Father than their earthly fathers are, and if they are dear to us, they are far dearer to Him. We cannot do anything better for them than to trust them to His care and hardly anything worse than to try to keep them as our own. We must make up our minds to move into our dwelling place in God and to take there with us all our possessions—above all, those we love.

Hannah Whitall Smith

JULY 16—HEAVEN'S LOVED INHABITANTS

Blessed the guest at home in your place! We expect our fill of good things in your house,
your heavenly manse. Psalm 65:4 TM

I remember when, after being away from home some time, I went back to see my honored mother. I thought in going back I would take her by surprise and come in unexpectedly upon her. I went into one room and then into another, and I went all through the house, but I could not find that loved mother. When I was told she had gone away, the old place didn't seem like home at all. Home had lost its charm to me. It was my mother who made home so sweet to me. It is the loved ones who make home so sweet to everyone. It is the loved ones who are going to make heaven so sweet to all of us. Christ is there, God the Father is there, and many, many who were dear to us who lived on earth are there—and we shall be with them by and by.

Dwight Lyman Moody

Entirely out of place is obscene, silly, and vulgar talk;
but instead, let there be thanksgiving.
Ephesians 5:4 NRSV

What would Jesus do as editor of a daily newspaper?

He would never allow a sentence or a picture in His paper that could be called bad, coarse, or impure in any way. He would probably conduct the political part of the paper from the standpoint of nonpartisan patriotism, always looking upon all political questions in the light of their relation to the kingdom of God and advocating measures from the standpoint of their relation to the welfare of the people, always on the basis of "What is right?" never on the basis of "What is for the best interests of this or that party?"

The end and aim of a daily paper conducted by Jesus would be to do the will of God. That is, His main purpose in carrying on a newspaper would not be to make money or gain political influence. But His first and ruling purpose would be to so conduct His paper that it would be evident to all His subscribers that He was trying to seek first the kingdom of God by means of His paper. This purpose would be as distinct and unquestioned as the purpose of a minister, missionary, or any unselfish martyr in Christian work anywhere.

All questionable advertisements would be impossible.

As editor of a daily paper today, Jesus would give large space to the work of the Christian world. He would devote a page possibly to the facts of reform, of sociological problems, of institutional church work and similar movements.

Charles Sheldon

"Whoever does not love me does not keep my words; and the word that you hear is not mine, but is from the Father who sent me." John 14:23–24 NRSV

You women, if you found that your husband was giving his love and attention to some other woman, and if you saw that some other woman was encroaching on his mind and heart and was usurping your place and was pushing you out of the place, wouldn't you grieve? Don't you think that God grieves when you push Him out of your life? You don't treat God square. You businessmen don't treat God fair. You let a thousand things come in and take the place that God Almighty had. You blame God for things you have no right to blame Him for. He is not to blame for anything.

You judge God. The spirit loves the Bible; the devil loves the flesh. You never think of going out on the street without dressing. You would be arrested before you went a block. You never think of going without breakfast, do you? I bet there are multitudes who have come here without reading the Bible or praying for this meeting. You can measure your desire for salvation by means of the amount of self-denial that you are willing to practice for Jesus Christ.

Billy Sunday

JULY 19—THE LUSTER OF LOVE

Love the LORD, all you his saints. The LORD preserves the faithful, but abundantly repays the one who acts haughtily. Psalm 31:23 NRSV

Without love, all our religion is vain. It is not how much we do but how much we love. If a servant does not do his work willingly and out of love, it is not acceptable. Duties not mingled with love are as burdensome to God as they are to us. David therefore counsels his son Solomon to serve God with a willing mind. To do duty without love is not sacrifice but penance.

Love is a pure flame kindled from heaven. By it we resemble God, who is love. Believing and obeying do not make us to be like God, but by love we grow to be like Him. Love is a grace which most delights in God and is most delightful to Him. Love puts a flourishing and luster upon all the graces. The graces seem to be eclipsed, unless love shine and sparkle in them. Faith is not true, unless it works by love. The waters of repentance are not pure, unless they flow from the spring of love. Love is the incense that makes all our services fragrant and acceptable to God.

Thomas Watson

By day the LORD directs his love, at night his song is with me—
a prayer to the God of my life. Psalm 42:8 NIV

*L*ove is the divine element in life, because God is love and because he who loves is born of God; therefore, let us keep our friendships in repair. They are worth spending time over because they constitute so large a part of our lives. Let us cultivate this spirit of friendship that it may grow into a great love, not only for our friends but also for all humanity.

Those of you who are going to the mission field must remember that your mission will be a failure unless you cultivate this element of love. Two years ago I came to a remote island in the South Pacific. At one end of the island were a missionary and his wife. At the other end were another missionary and his wife. You would suppose they would see each other every day, but they were not on loving terms. They were on war terms. What was the trouble about? It was a quarrel over a word in the native language that they should use for "God" in their translation of the New Testament.

Henry Drummond

THE FATHER'S POWERFUL LOVE—JULY 21

The LORD loves those who hate evil; he guards the lives of his faithful;
he rescues them from the hand of the wicked. Psalm 97:10 NRSV

*W*e have often walked in the field in the early morning and have noticed how the rising sun has turned each dewdrop into a glittering gem. One ray of its own bright light makes a little sun of each of the million drops that hang from the pendent leaflets and sparkle everywhere. But it is helpful to remember that the glorious orb itself contains infinitely more light than all the dewdrops ever did or ever will reflect.

And so of our heavenly Father. He Himself is the great source of all that is noble and true and of all that ever has been loving and trustworthy. Each beautiful trait of each beautiful character is but the dim reflection of some ray of His own great perfection. And the sum total of all human goodness and tenderness and love is but as the dewdrops to the sun. How blessed then to confide in the infinite and changeless love of such a father as our Father in heaven!

Hudson Taylor

In love a throne will be established; in faithfulness a man will sit on it. . .
one who in judging seeks justice. Isaiah 16:5 NIV

*C*hrist our advocate tracks our cause and business in heaven as His great and primary design and business. It is as if our concerns were so attended to by Him there that all the glory and honor which is paid Him in heaven would not divert Him one moment from our business. He pleads the cause of believers by His blood. Unlike other advocates, it is not enough for Him to lay out only words, which is a cheaper way of pleading, but He pleads for us by the voice of His own blood. Every wound He received for us on earth is a mouth opened to plead with God on our behalf in heaven. No friend in the world is so generous and bountiful to this as Jesus Christ is to believers.

No friend in the world loves his friend with as impassioned and strong affection as Jesus Christ loves believers. There is no end of the account of Christ's love.

John Flavel

"Do not let your hearts be troubled. Trust in God; trust also in me." John 14:1 NIV

*I*f people really believed in the infinite love of God, what a change it would bring about! What is love? It is a desire to communicate oneself for the good of the object loved—the opposite to selfishness. The mother is willing to sacrifice herself for the good of her child. So God in His love is ever willing to impart blessing, and He is omnipotent in His love. This is true, my friends: God is omnipotent in love. He is doing His utmost to fill every heart. "But if God is really anxious to do that, and if He is Almighty, why does He not do it now?" You must remember that God has given you a will, and by the exercise of that will, you can hinder God and remain content with the low life of unbelief. Come now, and let us see the cause of the difference between God's high, blessed provision for His children and the low, sad experience of many of us in the unbelief that distrusts and grieves Him.

Andrew Murray

O Israel, hope in the LORD; for with the LORD there is unfailing love
and an overflowing supply of salvation. Psalm 130:7 NLT

In the face of all we know about the God of all comfort, you can realize with Job, David, Paul, and the saints of all ages that nothing else is needed to quiet all your fears but just this: that God is. Nothing can separate you from His love, absolutely nothing—neither death nor life, nor angels, nor principalities, nor powers, nor things present, nor things to come, nor height, nor depth, nor any other creature. Every possible contingency is provided for here. Not one of them can separate you from the love of God, which is in Christ Jesus our Lord.

After such a declaration as this, how can any of us dare to question or doubt God's love? Since He loves us, He cannot exist and fail to help us. We know by our own experience what a necessity it is for love to pour itself out in blessing on the ones it loves. Can we not understand that God who is love, who is, if I may say so, made out of love, simply cannot help blessing us? We do not need to beg Him to bless us; He simply cannot help it.

Hannah Whitall Smith

OUR BROTHER—JULY 25

For whosoever shall do the will of God, the same is my brother. Mark 3:35 KJV

If this is true, and it is, then the reverse is also true, and He is our Brother. The picture is given in the thirty-first and thirty-fourth verses: "There came then his brethren and his mother, and, standing without, sent unto him, calling him. . . . And he looked round about on them which sat about him, and said, Behold my mother and my brethren." How wonderful that He should graciously give this title to those who do the Father's will! And what is that will? The acceptance of His Son as our Savior and Lord and the submission of our will to His will as revealed in His Word, for His Word is His will. How near and dear He is to us, our Lord and our Brother! Hold it fast in your meditation—"Ours by faith; ours forever." Dear Lord, keep us in loving fellowship with Thyself this day. Amen.

Charles E. Hurlburt and T. C. Horton

July 26—Genuine Love

Above all, clothe yourselves with love. Colossians 3:14 NRSV

Suppose there were some young woman who, being poor and unable to buy real jewelry, bought imitation. She had a brass ring which she thought people would think was gold, but no one ever thought so. She had a string of white beads and thought people believed they were real pearls, but no one ever dreamed it. She had a pair of earrings with bits of glass and wished people to believe that they were real diamonds. Nobody ever thought such a thing.

After a while a young fellow falls in love with her. One night he says to her, "Mary, I wish you would throw away that brass ring and that white bead necklace and those pieces of brass and glass in your ears."

But she says, "Well, John, I love you, but I really cannot do it."

A few nights after, John comes again with a big leather box. Inside it are a real gold ring with two beautiful emeralds and a beautiful diamond, a necklace of real pearls, and genuine diamond earrings. "They are for you if you will throw away that brass and glass of yours."

How long do you think it would take Mary to throw away her imitation jewels? Men and women, cast all the baubles of this world's pleasures into the fire and receive the gold and emeralds and rubies and diamonds and pearls of heaven.

Reuben Archer Torrey

July 27—To Live Is to Love

And the grace of our LORD was exceeding abundant with faith and love which is in Christ Jesus. 1 Timothy 1:14 KJV

To love abundantly is to live abundantly, and to love forever is to live forever. Therefore, eternal life is inextricably bound up with love. We want to live forever for the same reason that we want to live tomorrow. Why do you want to live tomorrow? It is because there is someone who loves you, and whom you want to see tomorrow, be with, and love back. There is no other reason why we should live on than that we love and are beloved. No worse fate can befall a man in this world than to live and grow old alone, unloving, and unloved. So long as he has friends—those who love him and whom he loves—he will live, because to live is to love. Love must be eternal. It is what God is. Love is life. Love never fails, and life never fails so long as there is love.

Henry Drummond

"Because the LORD loves his people, he has made you their king." 2 Chronicles 2:11 NIV

You have heard of Helen Keller who was born deaf, unable to speak, and blind. Until she was seven years of age, her life was an absolute blank. Nothing could go into that mind because the ears and eyes were closed to the outer world. Then they began to put in little bits of knowledge and bit by bit to educate her.

But they reserved the religious instruction for Phillips Brooks. When she was twelve years old, they took her to him, and he talked to her through the young lady who had been the means of opening her senses and who could communicate with her by the exceedingly delicate process of touch. Phillips Brooks began to tell her about God and what He had done and how He loves people and what He is to us.

The child listened very intelligently and finally said, "Mr. Brooks, I knew all of that before, but I did not know His name." Have you not often felt something within you that was not you, some mysterious pressure, some impulse, some guidance, something lifting you and impelling you to do that which you would not yourself ever have conceived of? Perhaps you did not know His name—it is God who works in you. If we can really build our life upon that great, simple fact, the first principle of religion which we are so prone to forget—that God is with us and in us—we will have no difficulty or fear about our future life.

Henry Drummond

Old Love—July 29

"Therefore with lovingkindness I have drawn you." Jeremiah 31:3 NKJV

The righteousness of Jesus Christ may properly be called an everlasting righteousness. Christianity, in one sense, is as old as the creation. All the saints who have been saved or who ever will be saved are all saved by the righteousness of Christ. It was through faith in Him that Abel was saved. It was through the sacrifice of Jesus Christ that Abraham was accepted and that all the prophets of old were accepted. Persons under the law and under the gospel are to be saved only through Christ; therefore, Christ's righteousness may properly be called an everlasting righteousness.

George Whitefield

July 30—First Love

We love him, because he first loved us. 1 John 4:19 KJV

*U*nder our first love, what promises did we make to Him? But how disobediently have we behaved ourselves in this covenant? How little have we reverenced Him? How little have we lived to His glory?

When commanded by Him to go work in His vineyard, we have often said, "We go, Lord." But we went not. Or if we did go, with what reluctance has it been? How unwilling to watch with our dear Lord and Master only one hour? And when His time of love was come, He entered into a covenant with us, and we became His. He washed us also with water and thoroughly washed us by His precious blood from the guilt of all our sins. In short, we were made exceedingly beautiful, and the kingdom of God was constructed in our hearts. But how we have fallen, who were once sons of the morning! How we have trusted in our own beauty, have grown spiritually proud, and provoked our patient and unspeakably long-suffering Lord to anger. Where is that ardent love we spoke of when we told Him that though we should die for Him, we would not deny Him in any wise?

George Whitefield

July 31—Tests of Love

The LORD your God is testing you to find out whether you love him with all your heart and with all your soul. Deuteronomy 13:3 NIV

*C*an we say we are filled with delight when we think on God?

Love desires familiarity and conversation. If we love God, we prize His ordinances because there we meet with God. He speaks to us in His Word, and we speak to Him in prayer. Let us examine our love to God. Do we desire intimacy of communion with God? Lovers cannot be long away from each other. Those who love God know not how to be away from Him. They can bear the want of anything but God's presence. They can do without health and friends, they can be happy without a full table, but they cannot be happy without God. What shall we say to those who can be all their lives long without God? Does that woman love her husband who cannot endure to be in his presence?

Thomas Watson

I will heal their backsliding, I will love them freely: for mine
anger is turned away from him. Hosea 14:4 KJV

*T*here is a great deal of difference between a willingness not to be condemned and a willingness to receive Christ for your Savior.

You tell of a willingness for deliverance, but what is the object of that willingness? It does not respect Christ. The inclination of your will goes no further than self; it never reaches Christ. You are willing not to be miserable; that is, you love yourself, and there your will and choice come to an end. It is but a vain pretense and delusion to say or think that you are willing to accept Christ.

Now if that willingness whereby you think you are willing to have Christ for a Savior is merely a forced thing, then your heart does not go out after Christ of itself. Instead you are forced and driven to seek an interest in Him. This forced compliance is not what Christ seeks of you. He seeks a free and willing acceptance. He seeks not that you should receive Him against your will but with a free will.

Jonathan Edwards

SOAR WITH LOVE—AUGUST 2

God loves the pure-hearted and well-spoken; good leaders also delight in their friendship.
Proverbs 22:11 TM

A stone is as likely to rise and fly in the air as our hearts are naturally to move toward heaven. You need not hinder the rocks from flying up to the sky. It is sufficient that you do not help them; and surely if our spirits have not great assistance, they may easily be kept from soaring upward. Think of this in the choice of your company! When your spirits are so predisposed for heaven that you need no help to lift them up, you may be less careful of your company. But until then, as you love the delights of a heavenly life, be careful.

How will it advantage you in a divine life to hear how the market goes or what news is stirring? What will it assist to the raising of your heart to hear some unimportant controversy? No, if you had been newly warming your heart in the contemplation of the blessed joys above, this discussion would benumb your affections and quickly freeze your heart again. People cannot well talk of one thing and mind another, especially things of such different natures.

Richard Baxter

August 3—Brave Love

...putting on the breastplate of faith and love; and for an helmet, the hope of salvation.
1 Thessalonians 5:8 KJV

As Jesus pleases him in prosperity, so in adversity Jesus is not displeasing to him. The wise lover regards not so much the gift of Him who loves as the love of Him who gives. He regards the affection of the giver rather than the value of the gift and sets his beloved above all gifts. The noble lover does not rest in the gift but in Jesus who is above every gift.

All is not lost, then, if you sometimes feel less devout than you wish toward Jesus. That good and sweet feeling which you sometimes have is the effect of present grace and a certain foretaste of your heavenly home. It is not an illusion that you are sometimes engrossed in intense joy and then quickly returned to the usual follies of your heart. For these are evils that you suffer rather than commit. So long as they displease you and you struggle against them, it is a matter of merit and not a loss.

Fight like a good soldier, and if you sometimes fall through weakness, rise again with greater strength than before, trusting in Christ's most abundant grace.

Thomas à Kempis

August 4—Know the Love of Christ

I led them with cords of human kindness, with bands of love. Hosea 11:4 NRSV

We see the love of Christ in that the human nature, the nature of man, is taken into union with God. By this very act of the heavenly wisdom, we have an inconceivable pledge of the love of Christ to man. He took into union with Himself our nature. What did it signify but that He intended to take into union with Himself our person. For this very purpose, He assumed our nature. In that flesh He died for us, the just for the unjust, that He might bring us to God.

We may yet see more of His love in that He is gone into heaven, there to make ready and to prepare for us our mansions as if we were the lords and He the servant! This is love!

He is now and has been ever since His ascension into glory laying out Himself as high priest for us. We also see yet more of His love by the fact that He will have us where He is, that we may see and be partakers of His glory.

John Bunyan

Honor everyone. Love the family of believers. 1 Peter 2:17 NRSV

I received a small sum of money with the following letter from one of the former orphans: "Beloved sir, once more it is the privilege of one of your former orphans to write you a few lines and ask your acceptance of this small offering of thanksgiving to God for all His loving-kindness to me and mine. I need hardly say that, as each year passes away, my respect for you and love for the dear place where I spent the best part of my childhood increases. I express my gratitude to the Father of the fatherless, who put it in the heart of you, His honored and beloved servant, to carry out such a noble scheme to the glory of God.

"How often, when tempted to indulge in the sin of unbelief, has the thought of my six years at the orphanage come across my mind like a gleam of sunshine. There the clothes I wore, the food I ate, the bed I slept on, and the walls around me were all in answer to believing prayer. What better prescription for any infidel than to go to the orphanage and inquire into its working!

"I pray that none of us orphans who have been sheltered there will be found wanting in that great day when we shall all stand around the throne of God. You, dear sir, will receive the reward of all your labors of love. May we all be there to thank you."

George Müller

LOVE OF GOD'S LAWS—AUGUST 6

"Woe to you Pharisees. . .you neglect justice and the love of God." Luke 11:42 NIV

*I*f you act as a Pharisee, you live outwardly the works of the law and judge them who fail to do so. Inwardly, in your heart, you wish that there were no law nor God to enforce the law if it were possible, so painful it is unto you to have your sinful appetites kept down. You teach another man not to steal when you are a thief in your heart and would steal if you could. You understand not the law right. It cannot be satisfied but with an unfeigned love.

The law is spiritual, and no person fulfills it except that by doing it through love from the bottom of the heart. The law is spiritual and will be both loved and fulfilled by a spiritual heart.

William Tyndale

If ye love me, keep my commandments. John 14:15 KJV

*O*ne of the evidences of perfect love is the realization that the impulse to Christian activities has changed from duty to delight. "I will run the way of thy commandments when thou shalt enlarge my heart." Instead of dragging himself to duty, there is a free, spontaneous impulse moving him to render with gladness any possible service to his Master—not from fear of the law, but from love to the Lawgiver. There is a point between the earth and the moon where gravitation changes. A projectile from earth, passing that point into the superior attraction of the moon, freely moves to meet it with ever-increased velocity. Thus, the believer, lifted by the power of the Holy Spirit out of the attraction of the world, under the stronger attraction of Christ, gravitates upward. He no longer needs a whip and spurs to urge him, but the magnetism of love draws him sweetly, yet mightily, onward toward the King in his beauty.

Daniel Steele

August 8—Advancing Love

"If you love those who love you, what credit is that to you?
Even 'sinners' love those who love them." Luke 6:32 NIV

*H*ow does your mind stand affected toward those who differ from you in their religious sentiments and practices? I do not say that Christian love will require you to think every error harmless. But to hate persons because we think they are mistaken, and to aggravate every difference in judgment or practice into a fatal error that destroys all Christian communion and love, is a symptom generally much worse than the evil it condemns.

Do you love the image of Christ in a person who thinks himself obliged in conscience to profess and worship in a manner different from yourself? Further, can you love and honor that which is truly amiable and excellent in those in whom much is defective, in those in whom there is narrowness of spirit, which may lead them perhaps to slight you? Can you love them as the disciples and servants of Christ who through a mistaken zeal may be ready to cast out your name as evil and to warn others against you as a dangerous person? Does your love show itself solid and sincere?

Philip Doddridge

The LORD will work out his plans for my life—
for your faithful love, O LORD, endures forever.
Psalm 138:8 NLT

*T*here is an experience that becomes more and more familiar to every-one who is trying to follow Christ—a feeling of the growing loneliness of his Christian life. It comes from a sense of the personal interest that Christ takes in him. It sometimes seems so strong, as if an unseen arm linked in his were taking him aside for a nearer intimacy and a deeper and more private fellowship. It is a humbling realization that God makes Himself as real to each poor unit as if he were the whole. Christ has died for others but in a particular sense for the individual. God has a love for all the world but a particular love for each person.

If I have God's will in my character, my life may become great and good. It may be useful and honorable. God has a life plan for every human life.

Henry Drummond

ONE SHEPHERD—AUGUST 10

And other sheep I have, which are not of this fold;
them also I must bring, and they shall hear my voice;
and there shall be one fold, and one shepherd. John 10:16

*I*srael had a limited view of our Christ. They were wrapped up in them-selves. Selfish, narrow in their vision of the Messiah that was to come, they were without compassion, as we ourselves so often are, having no patience with those who differ from us. Not so our Lord. He had a heart bound-less in love; a soul longing for the children of men; looking forward into the future, seeing the hatred of the Jews (His own people) to the cross, the cruel death, and then the many sheep, washed in the same blood, filled with the same Holy Spirit of Life, folded in the one fold. Wonderful vision! Shepherd of our lives, enlarge our hearts in sympathy with the puls-ings of Thine own loving heart. Amen.

Charles E. Hurlburt and T. C. Horton

August 11—Suitable Friend

A friend loves at all times, and kinsfolk are born to share adversity. Proverbs 17:17 NRSV

*C*an you love a little shining earth, a walking piece of clay? More so, can you love that God, that Christ, that glory, which are so truly and unmeasurably lovely? You can love your friend because he loves you. But is the love of friends like the love of Christ? Their weeping or bleeding for you do not ease your pain or stop the course of your tears or blood. But the tears and blood that fell from your Lord have an effective and healing quality. If love should foster love, what incomprehensible love is here before you! Pour out all the reserve of your affections here, although all is too little.

Who is more suitable for our love than Christ? His Godhead and humanity, His fullness and freeness, His willingness and constancy, all proclaim Him your most suitable friend. Although your eyes have never seen your Lord, yet you have heard His voice, received His benefits, and lived close to His heart. He taught you to know yourself and Him. He opened that first window through which you saw into heaven.

Richard Baxter

August 12—Supported by Love

When I thought, "My foot is slipping," your steadfast love, O LORD, held me up. Psalm 94:18 NRSV

*T*he work of God does not mean so much man's work for God as God's own work through man.

Many circumstances connected with my own early life and service presented this aspect of work vividly to me. As I think of some of them, I am reminded of how much the cause of missions is indebted to many who are never themselves permitted to see the mission field. Many, it may be, who are unable to give largely of their substance and who will be not a little surprised in the Great Day to see how much the work has been advanced by their love, their sympathy, and their prayers.

For myself and for the work that I have been permitted to do for God, I owe an unspeakable debt of gratitude to my beloved and honored parents, who have passed away and entered into rest but the influence of whose lives will never pass away.

Hudson Taylor

So he [Paul] reasoned in the synagogue with the Jews and the God-fearing Greeks, as well as in the marketplace day by day with those who happened to be there. Acts 17:17 NIV

*M*onday, August 22, 1743 (London)—After a few of us had joined in prayer, about four o'clock I set out and rode easily to Snow Hill; where, the saddle slipping quite upon my mare's neck, I fell over her head, and she ran back into Smithfield. Some boys caught her and brought her to me again, cursing and swearing all the way. I spoke plainly to them, and they promised to amend their ways.

I was setting forward when a man cried, "Sir, you have lost your saddlecloth." Two or three more came to help me put it on, but these, too, swore at almost every word. I turned to one and another and spoke in love. They all took it well and thanked me much. I gave them two or three little books which they promised to read over carefully.

Before I reached Kensington, I found my mare had lost a shoe. This gave me an opportunity of talking closely for nearly half an hour both to the blacksmith and his assistant. I mention these little circumstances to show how easy it is to redeem every fragment of time (if I may so speak) when we feel any love to those souls for which Christ died.

John Wesley

LOVE IS GOD'S GIFT—AUGUST 14

Bear with each other and forgive whatever grievances you may have against one another. Forgive as the LORD forgave you. Colossians 3:13 NIV

*T*hink what liberty many Christians give to their tongues. They say, "I have a right to think what I like." When they speak about each other, when they speak about their neighbors, when they speak about other Christians, how often there are sharp remarks! God shut my mouth if I am not to speak in tender love. How often there are found among Christians who are banded together in work sharp criticism, sharp judgment, hasty opinion, unloving words, secret contempt of each other, and secret condemnation of each other! Just as a parent's love covers her children and delights in them and has the tenderest compassion with their foibles or failures, so there ought to be in the heart of every believer a tender love toward every brother and sister in Christ.

Andrew Murray

AUGUST 15—LOVE THAT DOES NOT FADE

Give thanks to the LORD, for he is good; his love endures forever. 1 Chronicles 16:34 NIV

Survey the human race. You will observe strength in one person, beauty in a second, faithfulness in a third, wisdom in a fourth. But you shall find none excelling in them all as Christ does. Bread has one quality, water another, raiment another, and medicine another. But none has them all in itself as Christ does. He is bread to the hungry, water to the thirsty, a garment to the naked, and healing to the wounded.

Take away Christ, and where is the loveliness of any enjoyment? The best creature comfort apart from Christ is but a broken and empty well. It cannot hold one drop of true comfort. It is as a beautiful image in the mirror: turn away the face, and where is the image? Riches, honors, and comfortable relations are sweet when the face of Christ smiles upon us through them; but without Him, they are empty trifles.

The beauty and loveliness of all other things are fading and perishing, but the loveliness of Christ is fresh for all eternity.

John Flavel

AUGUST 16—AFFECTION REJECTED

*"But while he was still far off, his father saw him and was filled with compassion;
he ran and put his arms around him and kissed him." Luke 15:20 NRSV*

Suppose a son has gone far away from the paths of obedience and virtue. He has had one of the best of fathers, but he would not hear his counsels. He had a wise and affectionate mother, but he sternly resisted all the appeals of her tenderness and tears. Despite the most watchful care of parents and friends, he would go astray. As one madly bent on self-ruin, he pushed on, reckless of the sorrow and grief he brought upon those he should have honored and loved.

At last the youth finds himself ruined in constitution, in fortune, and in good name. He has sunk far too low to retain even self-respect. Nothing remains for him but agonizing reflections on past folly and guilt.

Truth flashes upon his soul, his heart quails, and his conscience thunders condemnation. So it must be with every sinner when all his sins against God shall stand revealed before his eyes, and there shall be nothing left for him but intense and unqualified self-condemnation.

Charles Finney

Because Christ also suffered for us. . .that ye should follow his steps. 1 Peter 2:21 KJV

*O*f what Christian use was Rachel Winslow's talent of song? Was the best she could do to sell her talent for so much a month, go on a concert company's tour, dress beautifully, enjoy the excitement of public applause, and gain a reputation as a great singer? Was that what Jesus would do?

She said, "I have made up my mind to use my voice in some way so as to satisfy my own soul that I am doing something better than pleasing fashionable audiences or making money or even gratifying my own love of singing. I am going to do something that will satisfy me when I ask: 'What would Jesus do?' I am not satisfied and cannot be when I think of myself as singing myself into the career of a concert company performer.

"During the week I am going to sing at the White Cross meetings down in the Rectangle, the slum district. They use a tent. It is in a part of the city where Christian work is most needed. What have we done all our lives for the suffering, sinning side of the city of Raymond? How much have we denied ourselves or given of our personal ease and pleasure to bless the place in which we live or imitate the life of the Savior?"

Miss Winslow has chosen to give her great talent to the poor of the city. Her plans include a musical institute where choruses and classes in vocal music shall be a feature. She is enthusiastic over her lifework.

Charles Sheldon

LET LOVE SHINE—AUGUST 18

He is my loving God and my fortress, my stronghold and my deliverer, my shield, in whom I take refuge, who subdues peoples under me. Psalm 144:2 NIV

*H*e who loves God is never weary of serving Him. He is sure to dwell with God in heaven if he has God dwelling in his heart. So that to love God is the truest self-love. He who does not love God does not love himself.

Love to God evidences sincerity. To love God is a better sign of sincerity than to fear Him. Repentance is no better than flattery when it arises only from fear of God's judgments and has no love mixed with it.

Do you love God? Then you may be sure of God's love to you. As it is with burning glasses, if the magnifying glass can set a fire, it is because the sun has first shined upon it. So if our hearts burn in love to God, it is because God's love has first shined upon us.

Thomas Watson

August 19—Love Will Last

"Though the mountains be shaken and the hills be removed,
yet my unfailing love for you will not be shaken." Isaiah 54:10 NIV

*C*an you tell me anything that is going to last? Many things Paul did not choose to name. He did not mention money, fortune, and fame. Instead he picked out the great things of his time, the things the best people thought had something in them, and brushed them firmly aside. There is a great deal in the world that is delightful and beautiful; there is a great deal in it that is great and engrossing; but it will not last. All that is in the world—the lust of the eye, the lust of the flesh, and the pride of life—are but for a little while. The immortal soul must give itself to something that is immortal. And the only immortal things are these: Now abides faith, hope, love, but the greatest of these is love.

Henry Drummond

August 20—God's Gift of Love

"If God were your Father, you would love me, for I came from God and now I am here.
I did not come on my own, but he sent me." John 8:42 NRSV

*T*he one great work of God's love for us is that He gives us His Son. In Him, we have all. The one great work of our heart must be to receive Jesus who has been given to us and to consider Him and use Him as ours. I must begin every day anew with the thought, I have Jesus to do all for me. In all weakness, darkness, or danger, and in the case of every desire or need, let your first thought always be, I have Jesus to make everything right for me because God has given Him to me. Let this always be your first thought: The Father has given me Jesus to care for me.

For this purpose, consider this gift of God every day as yours. Take Him new every day. Through faith, you have the Son. The love of God has given the Son. Take Him and hold Him fast in the love of your heart.

Andrew Murray

"Truly I tell you, wherever the gospel is proclaimed in the whole world, what she has done will also be told as a memorial to her." Mark 14:9 ISV

*I*n the days of our Lord's life on earth, when the shadow of the cross was already upon Him, one only amongst all His followers, a woman— Mary—had understood and really taken in His repeated declaration of the sufferings that awaited Him. When she came to anoint Him before- hand for the burial and broke the precious alabaster box she had reserved for this very purpose, the thief who kept the bag had only angry words of criticism and reproach. How sweet to her wounded spirit was her Master's commendation, "She hath done what she could!"

There is a day coming in which before assembled worlds He will make manifest the loving gifts and the secret service of His redeemed ones.

Hudson Taylor

COMFORTING LOVE—AUGUST 22

Be of good comfort, be of one mind, live in peace; and the God of love and peace will be with you. 2 Corinthians 13:11 NKJV

*T*wo little girls were talking about God, and one said, "I know God does not love me. He could not care for such a teeny, tiny little girl as I am."

"Dear me, sis," said the other little girl, "don't you know that is just what God is for—to take care of teeny, tiny little girls who can't take care of themselves, just like us?"

"Is He?" said the first little girl. "I did not know that. Then I don't need to worry anymore, do I?"

If any troubled, doubting heart should read these lines, then let me tell you again in trumpet tones that this is just what the Lord Jesus Christ is for—to care for and comfort all who mourn. All who mourn, all who are cast down—I love to think of such a mission of comfort in a world of mourning like ours; and I long to see every cast down and sorrowing heart comforted with this comforting of God.

Hannah Whitall Smith

August 23—Tender Love

"For the Lord disciplines those whom he loves, and chastises every child whom he accepts."
Hebrews 12:6 NRSV

*S*ometimes everything seems so firmly established in prosperity that no dream of disaster disturbs us. Our reputation is assured, our efforts have all been successful beyond our hopes, and our soul is at ease. The need for God is in danger of becoming far off and vague. Then the Lord is obliged to put an end to it all, and our prosperity crumbles around us like a house built on sand.

We are tempted to think He is angry with us. But in truth, it is not anger but tender love. His very love compels Him to take away the outward prosperity that is keeping our souls from entering the interior spiritual kingdom for which we long. When the fig tree ceases to blossom and there is no fruit in the vines, when the flock shall be cut off from the fold and there shall be no herd in the stalls, then, and often not until then, will our souls learn to rejoice in the Lord only and to joy in the God of our salvation.

Hannah Whitall Smith

August 24—Love from a Height

God will send forth his steadfast love and his faithfulness. Psalm 57:3 NRSV

*Y*ou and I sometimes dwell upon the love of Christ to give up heaven for us. We look at Him in the courtyard of Pilate, fastened to the whipping post with His bare back exposed to the lash of the Roman soldier. We look at Him as the lash cuts into His back again, again, and again until it is all torn and bleeding. Oh, how He loves us!

But looking down from the throne in heaven was God, and every lash that cut the back of Christ cut the heart of God. We see the soldiers with the crown of thorns, pressing it on His brow, and we see the blood flowing down. Oh, how He loved us! But every thorn that pierces His brow pierced also the heart of God. Through that awful day we see Him on the cross. We hear the last cry. We see how He loved us. But looking down from the throne of light and glory was God, and every nail that pierced His hands and feet pierced the heart of God.

What are you going to do about this love?

Reuben Archer Torrey

For I knew that thou art a gracious God, and merciful, slow to anger, and of great kindness.
Jonah 4:2 KJV

*B*ad temper! A lady came to me and said, "Mr. Sunday, I know I have a bad temper, but I am over with it in a minute." So is the shotgun, but it blows everything to pieces.

You abuse the receptionist because she doesn't connect you in a minute. I say you abuse your wife; you go cussing around if supper isn't ready on time, cussing because the coffee isn't hot. You dig your fork into a hunk of beefsteak and put it on your plate, and then you say: "Where did you get this, in the harness shop? Take it out and make a hinge for the door."

Then you go to your store or office and smile, and everybody thinks you are an angel about to sprout wings and fly to the imperial realm above. You growl at your children. You snap and snarl around the house until they have to go to the neighbors to see a smile. They never get a kind word.

You say, "Mr. Sunday, the church is full of hypocrites." So's hell. I say to you: If you don't want to go to hell and live with that whole bunch forever, come into the church where you won't have to associate with them very long. There are no hypocrites in heaven.

Billy Sunday

LOVE GROWN DARK—AUGUST 26

Woman, behold thy son! John 19:26 KJV

I remember a very promising young man whom I had in Sunday school in Chicago. His mother took in washing to educate her four children. This was her eldest son, and I thought that he was going to redeem the whole family. One day he stood with his mother at the cottage door—it was a poor house because she could not pay for their schooling, feed and clothe her children, and rent a very good house, too. When they were talking, a young man from the high school came up the street. This boy walked away from his mother. The next day the young man asked, "Who was that I saw you talking to yesterday?"

He replied, "That was my washerwoman."

I thought, *Poor fellow!* He will never amount to anything. That was a good many years ago. He has gone down, down, down, and now he is just a miserable wreck. Of course he would go down. Ashamed of his mother who loved him and toiled for him and bore so much hardship for him!

Dwight Lyman Moody

And [Jesus] went down with [His parents], and came to Nazareth,
and was subject unto them. Luke 2:51 KJV

I heard of a poor woman who sent her boy to school and college. When he was to graduate, he wrote his mother to come, but she wrote back that she could not because she was so shabby that she was afraid he would be ashamed of her. He wrote back that he didn't care how she was dressed and urged her so strongly that she came.

The day came for his graduation, and he walked down the broad aisle with that poor mother dressed very shabbily and put her into one of the best seats in the house. To her great surprise, he was the valedictorian of the class. He won a prize, and when it was given to him, he stepped down, kissed his mother, and said, "Here, Mother, here is the prize. It is yours. I would not have had it if it had not been for you."

I have read of one custom in China: On every New Year's morning each man and boy is said to pay a visit to his mother, carrying her a present varying in value according to his station in life. He thanks her for all she has done for him and asks a continuance of her favor another year.

Dwight Lyman Moody

AUGUST 28—SEEK LOVE FOR ONE ANOTHER

Wondrously show your steadfast love, O savior of those who seek refuge
from their adversaries at your right hand. Psalm 17:7 NRSV

*I*n looking back upon my past life, I know not where to begin or where to end in making mention of the Lord's mercies. His long-suffering toward me in the days of my unrepentant life cannot be described. If, however, I have much reason to praise God for His mercies toward me in those days, I have more abundant reason to admire His gentleness, long-suffering, and faithfulness toward me since I have known Him. How can I sufficiently praise Him for this long-suffering? He has been always the same gracious, kind, loving father, friend, supporter, teacher, and comforter to me.

Let us seek to be faithful in the Lord and toward each other! Let us seek to love each other in the truth and for the truth's sake. It is comparatively easy to begin to love, but it requires much watchfulness not to grow weary in love when little or no love is returned. But as our gracious, faithful God, notwithstanding all our wavering, loves us without change, so should we, His children, love each other. Lord, help us to do so!

George Müller

"Because he loves me," says the LORD, "I will rescue him; I will protect him." Psalm 91:14 NIV

*T*wo Americans who were crossing the Atlantic met on Sunday to sing hymns. As they sang "Jesus, Lover of My Soul," one of them heard a rich and beautiful voice behind him. He looked around, and although he did not know the face, he thought that he knew the voice. When the music ceased, the man asked if he had not been in the Civil War. The man replied that he had been a Confederate soldier.

"Were you at such a place on such a night?" asked the first.

"Yes," he replied, "and a curious thing happened that night. I was posted on sentry duty in the edge of a wood. About midnight when everything was very still and I was feeling homesick and miserable and weary, I thought that I would comfort myself by praying and singing 'Jesus, Lover of My Soul.' A peace came down upon me, and through the long night I remember having felt no more fear."

"Now," said the other, "listen to my story. I was a Union soldier and was in the wood that night with a party of scouts. I saw you standing, although I did not see your face. My men had their rifles focused upon you waiting the word to fire, but when you sang the words 'Cover my defenseless head with the shadow of Thy wing,' I said, 'Boys, lower your rifles; we will go home.'"

Henry Drummond

OUR LOVE SHOWS GOD'S POWER—AUGUST 30

I declare that your steadfast love is established forever; your faithfulness is as firm as the heavens. Psalm 89:2 NRSV

*T*hink of the church at large. What divisions! Think of the different bodies. That there are differences of opinion does not trouble me. We do not have the same constitution, temperament, and mind. But how often hate, bitterness, contempt, separation, and unlovingness are caused by the truths of God's Word! Our doctrines have been more important than love. We often think we are valiant for the truth, and we forget God's command to speak the truth in love. The very dearest truths of God have become mountains that have separated us.

If we want to pray in power, and if we want to expect the Holy Spirit to come down in power, then we must enter into a covenant with God that we love one another with a heavenly love. Are you ready for that?

Andrew Murray

August 31—The One Who Hates Love

"He has blinded their eyes and hardened their heart, so that they might not look with their eyes, and understand with their heart and turn—and I would heal them." John 12:40 NRSV

*S*atan has an aptitude to alter all things. He can make God seem to be to us a most fierce and terrible destroyer. He can make Christ appear to be a terrible exactor of obedience. And most amazingly, Satan can steal His love. He can make supposed sins unpardonable and unpardonable ones appear as virtues. He can make the law to be received for gospel and cause that the gospel shall be thrown away as a fable. He can persuade that faith is fancy and that fancy is the best faith in the world. It is for this purpose that Christ bids us to continue in His love because the right knowledge and faith drives away all such confusion.

John Bunyan

September 1—What Would Jesus Do—The College President

Jesus answered. . ."You must follow me." John 21:22 NIV

*D*onald Marsh, president of Lincoln College, said, "What would Jesus do in my place? I have tried to satisfy myself by thinking that He would simply go on as I have done, attending to the duties of my college work, teaching the classes in ethics and philosophy. But I have not been able to avoid the feeling that He would do something more.

"I belong to a class of professional men who have always avoided the duties of citizenship. We have lived in a little world of literature and scholarly seclusion. I understand that our city officials are a corrupt, unprincipled set of men and thoroughly selfish so far as the affairs of city government are concerned. Yet all these years I have been satisfied to let other men run the municipality and have lived in a little world of my own, out of touch and sympathy with the real world of the people.

"What would Jesus do? My plain duty is to take a personal part in this coming election, go to the primaries, throw the weight of my influence, whatever it is, toward the nomination and election of good men, and plunge into the very depths of the entire horrible whirlpool of deceit, bribery, political trickery, and saloonism as it exists in the city of Raymond today.

"I would sooner walk up to the mouth of a cannon anytime than do this. I would so much prefer to remain quietly in my scholastic life with my classes. But this is my cross; I must take it up or deny my Lord."

Charles Sheldon

It is good to. . .declare your steadfast love in the morning, and your faithfulness by night.
Psalm 92:1–2 NRSV

*E*nter upon saving souls with the right intentions. Aim at the glory of God in the person's salvation. Do it not to get a name for yourself or to bring people to depend upon you. Do it in obedience to Christ and in imitation of Him. Extend His tender love to people's souls.

Let your appeal proceed from compassion and love. To jeer, scoff, and vilify are not likely ways to reform people or convert them to God. Go to poor sinners with tears in your eyes so they may see that you have earnest compassion for their case. Let them perceive it is the desire of your heart to do them good and that it is your love for their souls that forces you to speak. Say to them, "Friend, love will not permit me to see you perish. I seek nothing but your own happiness. You will have the gain and comfort if you come to Christ." If we were to go to every neighbor like this, what blessed fruit should we quickly see!

Richard Baxter

LOVE OF MONEY—SEPTEMBER 3

For the love of money is a root of all kinds of evil, and in their eagerness to be rich some have wandered away from the faith and pierced themselves with many pains. 1 Timothy 6:10 NRSV

*H*ow many a young fellow has come to me, and when I have urged him to come to Christ, he has said, "I believe it is a good thing, but I should have to give up my employment if I did"?

Two young ladies said to Mrs. Torrey, when they seemed to be very near a decision, "We cannot come to Christ. We are employed in a large shop, and our employer requires us to misrepresent the goods. We cannot do that and be Christians, can we?"

"No, you cannot," Mrs. Torrey replied, and the young ladies said, "If we don't, then we lose our positions." God pity the man or the merchant who requires his employees to lie! How sad it is that those young women were ready to choose their position and small salary in the place of Jesus Christ and life eternal!

Reuben Archer Torrey

Let no debt remain outstanding, except the continuing debt to love one another,
for he who loves his fellowman has fulfilled the law. Romans 13:8 NIV

*O*ur Lord speaks of His relationship to us as the rule of our love to others: "Love one another, as I have loved you." But is it a vain thing to imagine that we can keep His commandments and love others, even as He kept His Father's and loved us? . . . Undoubtedly, if we seek to carry out the injunction in our strength, or without a full understanding of the truth of Jesus as the vine and us as its branches.

It is not the question of what we feel able to accomplish but of what Christ is able to work in us. We need to be brought to an entirely new mode of life—with the surrender to be cleansed from all that is of self and detached from all that is in the world, to live only and wholly as Christ lived for the glory of the Father.

Christ showed us that His love was the same love with which the Father had loved Him. Christ and His love are inseparable; they are identical. God is love, and Christ is love. God and Christ and the divine love can only be known by having them, by their life and power working within us. Our Lord gave His life for us as proof of His friendship. He gave His life to secure a place for His love in our hearts to rule us.

Andrew Murray

September 5—The Gospel Feast

And the angel said to me, "Write this: Blessed are those who are
invited to the marriage supper of the Lamb." Revelation 19:9 NRSV

*M*any of you, perhaps, are not hungry. Feeding upon past experiences will not satisfy our souls any more than what we did eat yesterday will sustain our bodies today. No, believers must look for fresh influences of divine grace and beg of the Lord to water them every moment. Come you to the marriage feast. You are as welcome now as ever. And may God set your souls longing for that time when we shall sit down and eat bread in the kingdom of heaven! There we shall have full measure of divine love and enjoy the glorious Emmanuel forevermore.

George Whitefield

Love Sees the Bright Side—September 6

[Love] always hopes. 1 Corinthians 13:7 NIV

*H*e who loves will rejoice in the truth. He will rejoice not in what he has been taught to believe, not in this church's doctrine or in that, not in this ism or in that ism, but in the truth. He will strive to get at facts. He will search for truth with a humble and unbiased mind and cherish whatever he finds. Love for truth includes the self-restraint which refuses to take advantage of others' faults; the charity which delights not in exposing the weakness of others; the sincerity of purpose that endeavors to see things as they are and rejoices to find them better than suspicion feared.

Henry Drummond

Triumph of Love—September 7

For in Christ Jesus. . .the only thing that counts is faith working through love.
Galatians 5:6 NRSV

*I*f we love God, we have all winds blowing for us, and everything in the world shall conspire for our good. We know not what trials we may meet with, but to them who love God, all things shall work for good. Every wind shall blow us to the heavenly port. Our cross shall make way for a crown.

The lack of love to God is the cause of desertion. The seed in the parable which had no root fell away. A person who has not the love of God rooted in his heart will fall away in time of temptation. He who loves God will cling to Him. That soldier who has no love to his commander will leave him when he sees an opportunity and run over to the enemy's side.

What shall we do to love God? Study God. If we would study Him more, we will love Him more. Take a view of His superlative excellencies, His holiness, His incomprehensible goodness. Make it your earnest request to God that He will give you a heart to love Him. This is an acceptable request; surely God will not deny it. He will pour of His Spirit upon you, whose golden oil shall make the lamp of your love burn bright.

Thomas Watson

September 8—Love in Heaven

The faith and love that spring from the hope that is stored up for you in heaven and that you have already heard about in the word of truth. Colossians 1:5–6 NIV

I enjoy my parents and my near and beloved friends with some delight. When I have given my whole heart to my friend, how sweet was that exercise of my love! What will it then be to live in the perpetual love of God! To see a family live in love with husband and wife, parents and children doing all in love to one another, and to see a town live together in love without any envyings, brawlings, contentions, lawsuits, or divisions; but every man loving his neighbor as himself, thinking they can never do too much for one another but striving to go beyond each other in love—how happy, how delightful a sight is this!

What blessed fellowship will the family of heaven be where there is no division nor differing judgments, no resentment, no deceitful friendship, no, not one unkind expression, not an angry look or thought; but all are one in Christ who is one with the Father, and all live in the love of Him who is love Himself! How near then will my soul be united to God! I shall so heartily, strongly, and incessantly love Him! Ah, my wretched heart can think of such a day and work and life with such joy! But my future enjoyments will be even livelier.

Richard Baxter

September 9—The Loving Servant

...but through love be servants one to another. Galatians 5:13 ASV

I f you have wealth, do not glory in it, nor in friends because they are powerful, but instead glory in God who gives all things, and who desires above all to give Himself. Do not boast of personal stature or of physical beauty, qualities that are marred and destroyed by a little sickness. Do not take pride in your talent or ability, for fear that you will displease God to whom belongs all the natural gifts that you have.

Do not think yourself better than others lest, perhaps, you be accounted worse before God who knows what is in man. Do not take pride in your good deeds, for God's judgments differ from those of men, and what pleases them often displeases Him. If there is good in you, see more good in others so that you may remain humble. It is very harmful to think yourself better than even one. The humble live in continuous peace, while in the hearts of the proud are envy and frequent anger.

Thomas à Kempis

For I wrote to you out of great sorrow and anguish of heart—along with many tears—not to make you sad but to let you know how much love I have for you. 2 Corinthians 2:4 ISV

Where there is love to God, there is a grieving for our sins of unkindness against Him. A child who loves his father cannot but weep for offending him. I must not abuse the love of so dear a Savior! Did not my Lord suffer enough upon the cross, but must I make Him suffer more? Shall I give Him more gall and vinegar to drink? How have I grieved His Spirit, trampled upon His royal commands, slighted His blood! This opens a vein of godly sorrow and makes the heart bleed afresh.

Peter thought how he was taken up into the mount of transfiguration where Christ showed him the glory of heaven in a vision. That he should deny Christ after he had received such striking love from Him, this broke his heart with grief. He went out and wept bitterly.

Let us test our love to God. Do we shed the tears of godly sorrow? Do we grieve for our unkindness against God, our abuse of mercy, our lack of improvement of talents? How far are they from loving God who sin daily and their hearts never smite them! They have a sea of sin and not a drop of sorrow.

Thomas Watson

LOVE DOES NOT COMPLAIN—SEPTEMBER 11

Be hospitable to one another without grumbling. 1 Peter 4:9 NKJV

I remember hearing of a dear girl who was obliged to undergo a serious and very painful treatment for some disease, and the doctors had dreaded the thought of her groans and outcries. But to their amazement not even a moan escaped her lips, and all the time she smiled at her father, who was present, and uttered only words of love and tenderness. The doctors could not understand it. When the worst was over, one of them asked how it could have been. She said, "I knew how much my father loved me, and I knew how he would suffer if he saw that I suffered, so I tried to hide my suffering. I smiled to make him think I did not mind."

Can any of us do this for our heavenly Father?

Hannah Whitall Smith

If ye love me, keep my commandments. John 14:15 KJV

*S*ome people seem to feel that they must be on probation and must prove that to love God is to love His character. For instance, God is Purity. And to be pure in thought and look, to turn away from unhallowed books and conversation, to abhor the moments in which we have not been pure, is to love God. God is Love; and to love men till private attachments have expanded into a philanthropy which embraces all—at last even the evil and enemies with compassion—that is to love God. God is Truth. To be true, to hate every form of falsehood, to live a brave, true, real life—that is to love God. God is Infinite; and to love the boundless reaching on from grace to grace, adding charity to faith, and rising upwards ever to see the Ideal still above us, and to die with it unattained, aiming insatiably to be perfect even as the Father is perfect—that is to love God.

F. W. Robertson

SEPTEMBER 13—LOVE FOR RICH AND POOR

Those who despise their neighbors are sinners, but happy are those who are kind to the poor. Proverbs 14:21 NRSV

*L*ove your neighbor. Perhaps he rolls in riches and you are poor and living in your little hut beside his lordly mansion. Do not covet his wealth and think no hard thoughts concerning him. Be content with your own lot, if you cannot better it, but do not look upon your neighbor and wish that he were as yourself. Love him, and then you will not envy him.

Perhaps, on the other hand, you are rich, and near you resides the poor. Agree that you are bound to love them. God has made of one blood all people who dwell upon the face of the earth. Take heed that you love your neighbor although he is in rags or sunken in the depths of poverty.

But perhaps you say, "I cannot love my neighbors because for all I do they return ingratitude and contempt." So much the more room for the heroism of love. If your neighbors are hard to please, seek not to please them but to please God. Love your neighbor, for in so doing you are following the footsteps of Christ.

Charles Haddon Spurgeon

There is no fear in love; but perfect love casteth out fear. 1 John 4:18 KJV

A lady had been asked to speak at a rescue mission where there were a number of poor women. As she entered, she saw a woman sitting outside in deplorable condition and asked, "Who is that?"

The female supervisor answered, "She has been into the house thirty or forty times, and she has always gone away again. Nothing can be done with her. We have been waiting for you, and you have only an hour for your speech."

The lady replied, "No, this is of more importance." She went outside where the woman was sitting and said, "My sister, what is the matter?"

"I am not your sister" was the reply.

Then the lady laid her hand on her and said, "Yes, I am your sister, and I love you." She so spoke until the heart of the poor woman was touched. The conversation lasted some time, and those inside were waiting patiently. Ultimately the lady brought the woman into the room. She would not sit on a chair but sat down on a stool beside the speaker's seat. And that love touched the woman's heart. She had found one who really loved her, and that love gave access to the love of Jesus. I plead that God would begin with us now and baptize us with heavenly love!

Andrew Murray

LOVE AND THE NATURE OF FAITH—SEPTEMBER 15

I will sing of the LORD's great love forever; with my mouth I will make your faithfulness known through all generations. Psalm 89:1 NIV

The only bond which unites us with God is union with Christ. But the faith which unites us with Christ grows out of a genuine feeling, which is called love. The promise of God is "I shall make them to love Me."

We are said to be loved of God when we love Christ, because when we love Christ, we receive a pledge that God loves us as Father; whereas, before we loved Christ, He terrified us as a hostile judge.

I do not concede that the Spirit asks no more from us than what is within our ability. Rather, He shows us where we must turn when we lack the strength to obey Him. When we hear Christ exhort us to perseverance, we must not rely on our own energy and industry; we must rather pray to Him who commands us to confirm us in His love.

John Calvin

September 16—Claim God's Love

They that be whole need not a physician, but they that are sick. Matthew 9:12 KJV

*H*ave you never tasted the luxury of indulging in hard thoughts against those who have injured you? What a positive fascination it is to brood over their unkindness, to pry into their malice, and to imagine all sorts of wrong things about them. It has made you wretched, of course, but it has been a fascinating sort of wretchedness that you could not easily give up.

Like this is the luxury of doubting. Things have gone wrong with you in your experience. What is more natural than to conclude that for some reason God has forsaken you and does not love you? How irresistible is the conviction that you are too wicked for Him to care for or too difficult for Him to manage. You do not mean to blame Him or accuse Him of injustice, for you feel that His indifference toward you is fully deserved because of your unworthiness. This ploy leaves you at liberty to indulge in your doubts under the guise of a just recognition of your own shortcomings.

The poor little lamb that has wandered from the flock and gotten lost in the wilderness might as well say, "The shepherd does not love me nor care for me nor remember me, because I am lost. He only loves and cares for the lambs that never wander." But Jesus says He came not to save the righteous but sinners. Your very sinfulness and unworthiness is your chief claim upon His love and His care.

Hannah Whitall Smith

September 17—Divided Love

"You cannot serve God and mammon." Luke 16:13 NKJV

*T*he road to heaven and the road to hell lead in different directions. Which master will you choose to follow? Be an out-and-out Christian. Him only shall you serve. Only in this way can you be well pleasing to God. Will you incur God's displeasure by rejecting Christ, too? He died to save you. Trust Him with your whole heart, for with the heart man believeth unto righteousness.

I believe that when Christ has the first place in our hearts—when the kingdom of God is first in everything—we shall have power, and we shall not have power until we give Him His rightful place. If we let some false god come in and steal our love away from the God of heaven, we shall have no peace or power.

Dwight Lyman Moody

The LORD my God will enlighten my darkness. Psalm 18:28 KJV

*H*e has an especial tenderness of love towards thee for that thou art in the dark and hast no light, and His heart is glad when thou dost arise and say, "I will go to my Father." For He sees thee through all the gloom through which thou canst not see Him. Say to Him, "My God, I am very dull and low and hard; but Thou art wise and high and tender, and Thou art my God. I am Thy child. Forsake me not." Then fold the arms of thy faith and wait in quietness until light goes up in the darkness. Fold the arms of thy Faith, I say, but not of thy Action: Bethink thee of something that thou oughtest to do, and go and do it, if it be but the sweeping of a room, or the preparing of a meal, or a visit to a friend. Heed not thy feelings: Do thy work.

George MacDonald

THE PATH OF LOVE—SEPTEMBER 19

All the paths of the LORD are steadfast love and faithfulness, for those who keep his covenant and his decrees. Psalm 25:10 NRSV

*C*hrist did not do His deeds to obtain heaven. Heaven was His already. He did them freely for our sakes and to bring the favor of God to us and us to God. No natural son does his father's will because he would be heir. He is already heir by birth. His father gave him that out of pure love before he was born. Servants work for hire, children for love. So a Christian acts freely, considering nothing but the will of God and the value he can give his neighbor.

A gentle pastor, Jesus brings the Spirit of God, which loosens the bonds of Satan and couples us to God and His will through strong faith and fervent love. The poor and wretched sinner feels so great mercy, love, and kindness in God that he is sure in himself that it is not possible for God to forsake him or withdraw His mercy and love. He boldly cries out with Paul, saying, "Who shall separate us from the love that God loves us with?" In all tribulations, a Christian perceives that God is His Father and loves him even as he loved Christ.

William Tyndale

September 20—Light and Love

"And this is the judgment, that the light has come into the world, and people loved darkness rather than light because their deeds were evil." John 3:19 NRSV

$\mathcal{M}$an has no possibility of attaining to any heavenly perfection and happiness except in the way of the gospel. There is no possibility of any other way because there is nothing that can possibly change the first properties of life into a heavenly state. Therefore the "Word was made flesh" and must of all necessity be made flesh if man is to have a heavenly nature.

Now as all evil, sin, and misery have no beginning nor power of working but in their divided, contrary properties, so it is certain that man has nothing to turn to, seek, or aspire after but the lost spirit of love. Therefore it is that God only can be his redeemer because God only is love, and love can be nowhere else but in God and where God dwells and works.

William Law

September 21—God Loves You

"Look at the birds of the air; they do not sow or reap or store away in barns, and yet your heavenly Father feeds them. Are you not much more valuable than they?" Matthew 6:26 NIV

$\mathcal{T}$rue humility accepts the love that is bestowed upon it and the gifts of that love with a meek and happy thankfulness, while pride shrinks from accepting gifts and is afraid to believe in the goodness of the one who gives them. Were we truly humble, we would accept God's love with thankful meekness.

It will sometimes look to us impossible that the Lord can love such disagreeable, unworthy beings as we feel ourselves to be. We must ignore these insinuations against the love of God as we would any insinuations against the love of our dearest friend. The fight to do this may sometimes be very severe. We must at once assert in definite words in our own hearts, and if possible aloud to someone, that God does love us. Our steadfast faith will unfailingly bring us, sooner or later, a glorious victory.

Hannah Whitall Smith

Where you are right now is God's place for you. Live and obey and
love and believe right there. 1 Corinthians 7:17 TM

*F*or one seeking Christian perfection, God is always in all his thoughts. And loving God, he loves his neighbor as himself. He cannot speak evil of his neighbor any more than he can lie either to God or man. He ceases not to pray for them although they reject his love.

Love has purified his heart from envy, malice, wrath, and every unkind temper. It has cleansed him from pride. And indeed all possible reasons for contention on his part are cut off. His one intention at all times and in all places is not to please himself but to please Him whom his soul loves.

All the commandments of God he accordingly keeps and that with all his might because his obedience is in proportion to his love. He continually presents his soul and body as a living sacrifice, holy, acceptable to God. Entirely and without reserve he devotes himself, all he has, all he is, to His glory. All the talents he has, every power and faculty of his soul, every member of his body, he constantly employs according to his master's will.

John Wesley

FEELINGS OF LOVE—SEPTEMBER 23

Learn to love appropriately. You need to use
your head and test your feelings. Philippians 1:9 TM

*C*hildren greet their father from the window as he turns the corner and comes down the street. He hears the rush of their feet along the hall as he inserts his latchkey in the door. But one day he begins to question whether they greet him for the love they bear for him or for the gifts with which he fills his pockets. One day, therefore, he gives them due notice that there will be no gifts when he returns at night. Their faces fall, but when the hour of return arrives, they are at the window as usual, and there is the same trampling of little feet to the door. "Ah," he says, "my children love me for myself," and he is glad.

Our Father sometimes cuts off the supply of joy and suffers us to hunger so that He may know what is in our hearts, and whether we love Him for Himself. If we still cling to Him, He is glad and restores comforts to His mourners with both hands.

F. B. Meyer

...so that you might have him back forever, no longer as a slave but more than a slave, a beloved brother. Philemon 15–16 NRSV

When I came, the chief presented me with a slave girl about ten years old. I thanked him and said that I thought it wrong to take away children from their parents. I wished him to give up this system altogether. He urged that she was to be a child to bring me water and that a great man ought to have a child for the purpose, yet I had none.

I replied that I had four children and should be very sorry if my chief were to take my little girl and give her away, and that I would prefer this child to remain and carry water for her own mother. He thought I was dissatisfied with her size and sent for one a head taller. After many explanations of the repugnance of slavery and how displeasing it must be to God to see His children selling one another and giving each other so much grief as this child's mother must feel, I declined her, also.

To take her away and probably never be able to secure her return would have produced no good effect on the minds of the natives. They would not then have seen evidence of our hatred to slavery.

All I can say in my solitude is: May heaven's rich blessing come down on everyone—American, English, Turk—who will help heal this open sore of the world.

David Livingstone

SEPTEMBER 25—VAIN LOVE

"But strive first for the kingdom of God and his righteousness, and all these things will be given to you as well." Matthew 6:33 NRSV

This is the greatest wisdom—to seek the kingdom of heaven through disdain of the world. It is vanity, therefore, to seek and trust in riches that perish. It is vanity, also, to court honor and to be puffed up with pride. It is vanity to follow the lusts of the body and to desire things for which severe punishment later must come. It is vanity to wish for long life and to care little about a well-spent life. It is vanity to be concerned with the present only and not to make provision for things to come. It is vanity to love what passes quickly and not to look ahead where eternal joy abides.

Try to turn your heart from the love of things visible, and bring yourself to love things invisible. For those who follow their own evil passions stain their consciences and lose the grace of God.

Thomas à Kempis

Finally, all of you, live in harmony with one another; be sympathetic,
love as brothers, be compassionate and humble. 1 Peter 3:8 NIV

*A*n advocate is one who pleads the cause of another, who uses his influence in behalf of another by his request. Unless he himself is clear of the crime of which the criminal is accused, an advocate is not the proper person to represent him before a throne of mercy.

Would you call a man your friend who wished you to commit murder or robbery, to tell a lie, or to commit any crime?

No! No man is a true friend of a sinner unless he is desirous that he should abandon his sins. If any person would have you continue in your sins, he is the adversary of your soul. Instead of being in any proper sense your friend, he is playing the devil's part to ruin you.

Christ is the compassionate friend of sinners, a friend in the best and truest sense. He does not sympathize with your sins, but His heart is set upon saving you from your sins. I said He must be the compassionate friend of sinners. His compassion must be stronger than death, or He will never meet the necessities of the case.

Charles Finney

PERSONAL KINDNESS—SEPTEMBER 27

Be ye kind one to another. Ephesians 4:32 KJV

*W*hat was the secret of such a one's power? What had she done? Absolutely nothing; but radiant smiles, beaming good-humor, the tact of divining what everyone felt and everyone wanted, told that she had got out of self and learned to think of others; so that at one time it showed itself in deprecating the quarrel, which lowering brows and raised tones already showed to be impending, by sweet words; at another by smoothing an invalid's pillow; at another, by soothing a sobbing child; at another, humoring and softening a father who had returned weary and ill-tempered from the irritating cares of business. None but she saw those things. None but a lovely heart could see them. That was the secret of her heavenly power. The one who will be found in trial capable of great acts of love is ever the one who is always doing considerate small ones.

F. W. Robertson

But speaking the truth in love, we must grow up in every way
into him who is the head, into Christ. Ephesians 4:15 NRSV

We love because He first loved us. Contemplate the love of Christ, and you will love. Stand before that mirror, reflect Christ's character, and you will be changed into the same image. There is no other way. You cannot love to order. You can only look at the lovely object and fall in love with it and grow into likeness of it. And so look at this perfect character, this perfect life. Look at the great sacrifice as He laid down Himself, all through life and upon the cross of Calvary, and you must love Him. And loving Him, you must become like Him.

Love generates love. It is a process of induction. Put a piece of iron in the presence of a magnetized body, and that piece of iron for a time becomes magnetized. It is charged with an attractive force in the mere presence of the original force. As long as you leave the two side by side, they are both magnets alike. Remain side by side with Him who loved us and gave Himself for us, and you, too, will become a center of power, a permanently attractive force; and like Him you will draw all people unto you, like Him you will be drawn unto all people. That is the inevitable effect of love. There is no mystery about it. We love others, we love everybody, we love our enemies because He first loved us.

Henry Drummond

SEPTEMBER 29—JESUS' GIFT OF LOVE

Christ loved the church and gave himself up for her. Ephesians 5:25 NRSV

The more I understand and contemplate Jesus' surrender of Himself for me, the more I give myself again to Him. The surrender is a mutual one. The love comes from both sides. His giving of Himself makes such an impression on my heart that my heart with the same love and joy becomes entirely His. I know that I have Jesus wholly for me and that He has me wholly for Him.

Through faith I live in Jesus who loved me and gave Himself for me. And I say, "No longer do I live, but Christ liveth in me." In His great love, the Father gave the Son. It was out of love that Jesus gave Himself. The taking, the having of Jesus is the entrance to a life in the love of God: This is the highest life. Through faith we must press into love and dwell there.

Andrew Murray

"He is good; his love endures forever." 2 Chronicles 5:13 NIV

One of the most illuminating names of God is the one especially revealed by our Lord Jesus Christ—the name of "Father." God had been called throughout the ages by many other names that expressed other aspects of His character. Christ alone has revealed Him to us under the all-inclusive name of *Father*—a name that holds within itself all other names of wisdom and power, and above all of love and goodness. The name embodies for us a perfect supply for all our needs. Christ, who was the only begotten Son in the bosom of the Father, was the only one who could reveal this name, for He alone knew the Father. "As the Father knoweth me," He said, "even so know I the Father."

It is inconceivable that a good father could forget or neglect or be unfair to his children.

Hannah Whitall Smith

LOVE IN THREE WORDS—OCTOBER 1

Whoever does not love does not know God, because God is love. 1 John 4:8 NIV

God is love" is the greatest sentence ever written. It sums up the whole contents of the Bible. If I were asked for a sentence to print in letters of gold on the outside of our Bible, a sentence that summed up the whole contents of the Book, it would be this one: "God is love." It is the subject of the first chapter of Genesis, it is the subject of the last chapter of Revelation, and it is the subject of every chapter that lies in between.

The Bible is simply God's love story, the story of the love of a holy God to a sinful world. There is mighty power in that one short sentence, power to break the hardest heart, power to reach individual men and women who are sunk down in sin and to lift them up until they are fit for a place beside the Lord Jesus Christ upon the throne.

Reuben Archer Torrey

October 2—Love Balances the Scale

"You have been weighed on the scales and found wanting." Daniel 5:27 NIV

In Matthew, the Bible tells us to love the Lord our God with all our heart, with all our soul, and with all our mind. This is the first and greatest commandment. How much do you weigh by that law? Put God first in everything—in business, in politics, in social life, in study, in everything. Do you do it? Have you always done it? No, you say, I have not. Then you are weighed and found wanting.

Every one of us is weighed and found wanting. What shall we do then? This is where the gospel comes in. God has weighed the whole world in the balance and found it wanting. In Christ He provided salvation for a wanting world. When we take Christ into the balance with us, then we are weighed and not found wanting.

Reuben Archer Torrey

October 3—Love and the Law

Love does no harm to its neighbor. Therefore love is the fulfillment of the law.
Romans 13:10 NIV

The Ten Commandments are not ten different laws. They are one law. If I am being held up in the air by a chain with ten links and I break one of them, down I come just as surely as if I break the whole ten. If I am forbidden to go out of an enclosure, it makes no difference at what point I break through the fence. The golden chain of obedience is broken if one link is missing.

If the love of God fills your heart, you will be able to fulfill the law. Love summarizes the Ten Commandments. Love to God will admit no other god. Love to God will never dishonor His name. Love to God will reverence His day. Love to parents makes one honor them. Hate, not love, is a murderer. Lust, not love, commits adultery. Love will give but never steal. Love will not slander or lie. Love's eye is not covetous.

Dwight Lyman Moody

Be humble and gentle. Be patient with each other,
making allowance for each other's faults because of your love. Ephesians 4:2 NLT

When our union with Christ is perfect in glory, then our joy will be full. He who loves Christ loves His appearing.

Love will stoop and submit to anything whereby it may be serviceable to Christ. As we see in Joseph of Arimathea and Nicodemus, both of them honorable persons, one takes down Christ's body with his own hands and the other embalms it with sweet odors. It might seem much for persons of their rank to be employed in that service, but love made them do it. If we love God, we shall not think any work too insignificant for us by which we may be helpful to Christ's members. Love is not squeamish. It will visit the sick, relieve the poor, wash the saints' wounds. The mother who loves her child will do those things for her child which others would scorn to do. He who loves God will humble himself to the most undignified task of love for Christ and His members.

Thomas Watson

Honor, Obey, Love—October 5

Children, obey your parents in the LORD: for this is right. Honour thy father and
mother; which is the first commandment with promise. Ephesians 6:1–2 KJV

If your parents are still living, treat them kindly. Do all you can to make their declining years sweet and happy. Bear in mind that this is the only commandment that you may not always be able to obey. As long as you live, you will be able to serve God and obey all the other commandments. But the day comes to most people when Father and Mother die. What bitter feelings you will have when the opportunity has gone by if you fail to show them the respect and love that is their due!

Joseph wasn't satisfied until he had brought his old father down into Egypt. He was the greatest man in Egypt next to Pharaoh. He was arrayed in the finest garments and had Pharaoh's ring on his hand and a gold chain about his neck. Yet when he heard Jacob was coming, Joseph hurried out to meet him. He wasn't ashamed of the man with his shepherd's clothes.

Dwight Lyman Moody

OCTOBER 6—THE LOVING FATHER

I will be a father to him, and he shall be a son to me. I will not take my steadfast love from him. 1 Chronicles 17:13 NRSV

*I*n our Lord's last prayer (John 17:1), He says that He has declared to us the name of the Father so we may discover the wonderful fact that the Father loves us as He loved His Son. Now which one of us really believes this? We have read this chapter, I suppose, more often than almost any other chapter in the Bible. Yet do any of us believe that it is an actual, tangible fact that God loves us as much as He loved Christ? If we believed this to be the case, could we ever have an anxious or rebellious thought again? We would be absolutely and utterly sure always, under every conceivable circumstance, that the divine Father who loves us just as much as He loved His only begotten Son would care for us in the best possible way. He could tell us emphatically not to be anxious about anything because He knew His Father and knew that it was safe to trust Him completely.

"Your heavenly Father," Jesus says, "cares for the sparrows and the lilies, and of course therefore He will care for you who are of so much more value than many sparrows." How supremely foolish it is for us to be worried about things, when Christ has said that our heavenly Father knows that we have need of all these things! For being a good Father, He must in the very nature of the case supply it, when He knows our need.

Hannah Whitall Smith

OCTOBER 7—LOVE AND CONTENTMENT

Whoever loves wealth is never satisfied with his income. Ecclesiastes 5:10 NIV

*C*ontentment is the very opposite of covetousness, which is continually craving for something it does not possess. Do not worry about the future because God has promised never to leave or forsake you. What does the child of God want more than this? I would rather have that promise than all the gold of the earth.

Is the covetous person ever satisfied with his possessions? Riches are like a mirage in the desert that has all the appearance of satisfying and lures the traveler on with the promise of water and shade. But the traveler only wastes his strength in the effort to reach it. Riches never satisfy. The pursuit of them always turns out to be a snare.

Dwight Lyman Moody

LOVE BEYOND LAW—OCTOBER 8

"You have loved righteousness and hated wickedness." Hebrews 1:9 NIV

*T*he scriptures reveal to us glimpses of the delight, satisfaction, and joy our Lord has in us. That we should need Him is easy to comprehend; that He should need us seems incomprehensible. That our desire should be toward Him is a matter of course, but that His desire should be toward us passes the bounds of human belief. And yet over and over He says it, and what can we do but believe Him?

At every heart He is continually knocking and asking to be taken in as the supreme object of love. In a thousand ways He makes this offer of oneness with Himself to every believer. But all do not say yes to Him. Other loves and other interests seem to them too precious to be cast aside. They miss an unspeakable joy.

You, however, are not one of these. From the very first, eagerly and gladly to all His offers your soul has cried out, "Yes, Lord, yes!" What to them is lawful, love has made unlawful for you. To you He can make known His secrets, and to you He looks for an instant response to every requirement of His love. Your love and devotedness are His precious reward for all He has done for you.

Hannah Whitall Smith

LOVE AND LAW—OCTOBER 9

For the LORD is righteous, he loves justice; upright men will see his face. Psalm 11:7 NIV

*I*t is a privilege to do the commandments. And as my soul trembles at the fearfulness of will, love comes with its calm power. Where God's law is, is God's love. Look at law—it withers your very soul with its stern, inexorable face. But look at love or look at God's will, which means look at love's will, and you are reassured, and your heart grows strong. God's will, then, is as great as God, as high as heaven—yet as easy as love. For love knows no hardness and feels no yoke.

Give me love, pure, burning love and loyalty to Him, and I shall climb from law to law through grace and glory to the place beside the throne where the angels do His will. There are two ways, therefore, of looking at God's will—one looking at the love side of it, the other at the law; the one ending in triumph, the other in despair; the one a liberty, the other a slavery.

Henry Drummond

147

OCTOBER 10—TEACH US HOW TO LOVE

"The Father himself loves you because you have loved me and
have believed that I came from God." John 16:27 NIV

*G*od's love, as displayed in Christ, teaches us what love is. The question is often asked, "How shall I love?" Look at the love of Christ and drink in its spirit. Man is prone to love himself supremely. But here is a totally different sort of love from that. This love commends itself in that while we were yet sinners, Christ died for us. How forcibly does this rebuke our selfishness! How much we need this lesson to subdue our narrow selfishness and shame our unbelief!

How strange it is that people do not realize the love of God! The wife of a minister who had herself labored in many revivals said to me, "I never, until a few days ago, knew that God is love. I never understood it in all its interconnections before."

I assure you, the love of Jesus is a great thing to see as it is! When love becomes a reality to the soul and you come under its powerful sympathy, then you will find in the gospel the power of God unto salvation.

Charles Finney

OCTOBER 11—LOVE AND SPIRITUAL SICKNESS

O taste and see that the LORD is good; happy are those who take refuge in him.
Psalm 34:8 NRSV

*W*hen Christians grow more in love with the world, it indicates a decrease of spiritual love. Their thoughts and interests are still bound to the earth. It is a sign they are going down the hill quickly and their love to God is declining. When rust attacks a metal, it takes away the brightness and corrodes the metal. In the same way, when the world clings to people's souls, it not only hinders the shining luster of their graces, but by degrees it corrodes them.

Love is a grace that Christians do not know how to be without. A soldier may as well be without his weapons, an artist without his pencil, a musician without his instrument, as a Christian without love. How careful then should we be to keep alive our love for God!

Thomas Watson

And if I have prophetic powers, and understand all mysteries and all knowledge, and
if I have all faith, so as to remove mountains, but do not have love, I am nothing.
1 Corinthians 13:2 NRSV

Love is the highest gift of God. All visions or revelations are little things compared to love.

Beware of judging people to be either right or wrong by your own feelings. Beware of thinking, "Because I am filled with love, I need not have so much holiness. Because I pray always, therefore I need no set time for private prayer. Because I watch always, therefore I need no particular self-examination." Let this be our voice: "I prize Your commandments above gold or precious stones. What love have I unto Your law!"

I appeal to you: Beware of bigotry. Beware of self-indulgence, yes, and making a virtue of it.

John Wesley

LOVE OF IDOLS—OCTOBER 13

"You shall not make for yourself an idol in the form of anything in
heaven above or on the earth beneath or in the waters below. You shall
not bow down to them or worship them." Exodus 20:4–5 NIV

Many a man makes an idol of his wife. Not that a man can love his wife any too much, but he can put her in the wrong place. He can put her before God. When a man regards his wife's pleasure before God's pleasure, when he gives her the first place and God the second place, his wife is an idol.

Many a woman makes an idol of her children. Not that we can love our children too much. The more dearly we love Christ, the more dearly we love our children, but we can put our children in the wrong place. We can put them before God and their interests before God's interests. When we do this, our children are our idols.

Many a man makes an idol of his reputation or his business. Reputation or business is put before God.

One great question for us to decide: Is God absolutely first? Is He before wife, before children, before reputation, before business, before our own lives?

Reuben Archer Torrey

OCTOBER 14—LOVE IN A LOCKET

If anyone says, "I love God," yet hates his brother, he is a liar. 1 John 4:20 NIV

*T*here once lived a young girl whose perfect grace of character was the wonder of those who knew her. She wore on her neck a gold locket that no one was ever allowed to open. One day in a moment of unusual confidence, one of her companions was allowed to touch its spring and learn its secret. She saw written these words: "Whom having not seen, I love." That was the secret of her beautiful life.

You all know what it is to be hungry for love. Your heart seems unsatisfied until you can draw something more toward you. There have been times when I have had an unspeakable heart-hunger for Christ's love. My sense of sin is never strong when I think of the law; my sense of sin is strong when I think of love. It is when drawing near the Lord Jesus Christ and longing to be loved that I have the most vivid sense of unsymmetry, of imperfection, of absolute unworthiness, and of my sinfulness. Character and conduct are never so vividly set before me as when in silence I bend in the presence of Christ, revealed not in wrath but in love to me. I never so much long to be lovely, that I may be loved, as when I have this revelation of Christ before my mind.

Henry Drummond

OCTOBER 15—CHARITY OF THE SOULS

Let him know, that he who converteth a sinner from the error of his way shall save a soul from death, and shall cover a multitude of sins. James 5:20 ASV

*W*e may have a great deal of charity and concern for the bodies of our fellow creatures yet have no thought or concern for their immortal souls: But, oh, how sad is it to have charity for the body of our fellow creatures while we have no concern for their immortal souls. You may love to spend a merry evening with them, but you cannot bear the thought of going to a sermon or a religious society with them.

You will be so uncharitable as to join hand in hand with those who are hastening to their own damnation, while you will not be so charitable as to assist them in being brought from darkness to light and from the power of Satan unto God. Therefore let me advise you to be charitable to the souls of one another; that is, by advising them with all love and tenderness to follow after Christ and the things which belong to their immortal peace before they be forever hid from their eyes.

George Whitefield

Let no one despise your youth, but set the believers an example in speech and conduct,
in love, in faith, in purity. 1 Timothy 4:12 NRSV

*B*e an example in spirit. Always cherish a meek, gentle, and quiet spirit—a humble, loving, heavenly, and praying spirit. Such a spirit will almost silence the tongue of slander or cause its poisoned darts to fall harmless at your feet. Be an example in faith; prove to all by your works, your zeal, and labors of love that you heartily believe what you profess and teach to others. To teach the truth in a dull style lessens the force of truth and pours contempt upon its glory. But the truth presented in the spirit of faith will have a different effect on the hearers. Be an example in purity—purity of heart and life. Avoid impurity in word and action as well as in thought. In all things show yourself a pattern in every good work.

Serve God and pray for the promise of the Spirit. Then will you love your God and Savior. Then you will love your fellow Christians who bear the image of God. Then you will have the spirit of Jesus to love the fallen world and, like Him, to sacrifice all for their salvation.

Barton W. Stone

Courageous Love—October 17

I took courage, for the hand of the LORD my God was upon me, and I
gathered leaders from Israel to go up with me. Ezra 7:28 NRSV

*H*e who is afraid to own Christ has but little love to Him. As the sun expels fogs and vapors, so divine love in a great measure expels fear. Does he love God who can hear His blessed truths spoken against and be silent? He who loves his friend will stand up for him and vindicate him when he is reproached. Love animates a Christian. It fires his heart with zeal and steels it with courage.

Many, being drunk with the wine of prosperity, when the honor of God is wounded and His truths lie bleeding, are not affected by it. If we love God, our hearts ache for the dishonor done to God by wicked men. To see the banks of religion broken down and a flood of wickedness coming in, if there be any love to God in us, we shall lay these things to heart.

Thomas Watson

OCTOBER 18—POWER OF PURE LOVE

Hearken, my beloved brethren; did not God choose them that are
poor as to the world to be rich in faith, and heirs of the kingdom
which he promised to them that love him? James 2:5 ASV

Jesus has always many who love His heavenly kingdom, but few who bear His cross. He has many who desire consolation, but few who care for trial. He finds many to share His table, but few to take part in His fasting. All desire to be happy with Him; few wish to suffer anything for Him. Many follow Him to the breaking of bread, but few to the drinking of the cup of His suffering. Many honor His miracles, but few approach the shame of the Cross. Many love Him as long as they encounter no hardship. Many praise and bless Him as long as they receive some comfort from Him. But if Jesus hides Himself and leaves them for a while, they fall either into complaints or into deep dejection.

Those, on the contrary, who love Him for His own sake and not for any comfort of their own, bless Him in all trial and anguish of heart as well as in the bliss of consolation. Even if He should never give them consolation, yet they would continue to praise Him and wish always to give Him thanks. What power there is in pure love for Jesus—love that is free from all self-interest and self-love!

Thomas à Kempis

OCTOBER 19—WOMEN TEACH LOVE

By faith Moses, when he was come to years, refused to be called the son of
Pharaoh's daughter; Choosing rather to suffer affliction with the people of God,
than to enjoy the pleasures of sin for a season. Hebrews 11:24–25 KJV

Womanhood is a wonderful thing. In womankind we find the mothers of the race. There is no man so great, nor none sunk so low, but once he lay a helpless, innocent babe in a woman's arms and was dependent upon her love and care for his existence. It is woman who rocks the cradle of the world and holds the first affections of mankind. She possesses a power beyond that of a king on his throne. There was the ancient Jochebed who received the infant Moses from the hand of Pharaoh's daughter, and in a few short years she had him taught so to love his people and the God of his people that when he came to man's estate he chose rather to suffer affliction with the people of God than to enjoy the honor of being the grandson of the king.

Mabel Hale

"In everything do to others as you would have them do to you;
for this is the law and the prophets." Matthew 7:12 NRSV

*B*e sure that you look on your children as the gifts of God.

Parents, be warned. If your children disobey and violate the rules of your home, you must insist on penitence, confession, and apology. The relaxation of the bonds of authority in our homes is one of the saddest symptoms of national decay.

You must show yourself worthy to lead and rule your home. Your character must be such as to command respect. Those whom God has put into your charge require that you do not use your authority for selfish or capricious ends. Above all, love is the source of the truest authority. We count nothing hard or irksome that we do for those we love. Show love, and you will win love; and on love will be built respect, reverence, and obedience. Christ's golden rule holds good in every phase of life.

F. B. Meyer

LOVE THAT UNSETTLES US—OCTOBER 21

For I the LORD love justice, I hate robbery and wrongdoing. Isaiah 61:8 NRSV

*I*f love sees those it loves going wrong, it must because of its very love do what it can to save them. The love that fails to do this is only selfishness. Therefore, just because of His unfathomable love, the God of love, when He sees His children resting their souls on things that can be shaken, must necessarily remove those things from their lives so that they may be driven to rest only on the things that cannot be shaken. This process of removing is sometimes very hard.

When we talk of building upon the rock of Christ, we need to be shaken from off every other foundation in order that we may be forced to rest on the foundation of God alone. And this explains the necessity for those shakings. The Lord sees that we are building our spiritual houses on flimsy foundations, which will not be able to withstand the storms of life. Not in anger but in tender love, He shakes our earth until all that can be shaken is removed and only those things on a firm foundation are left behind.

Hannah Whitall Smith

October 22—First Love, Last Love

"I know your deeds, your love and faith, your service and perseverance,
and that you are now doing more than you did at first." Revelation 2:19 NIV

*L*ook back through all your experiences and think of the ways that
the Lord your God has led you and how He has fed and clothed you every
day. Think of how His grace has been sufficient for you in all your troubles.
His blood has been a pardon to you in all your sins. His rod and His staff
have comforted you.

When you have looked back upon the love of the Lord, then let faith
survey His love in the future, for remember that Christ's covenant and
blood have something more in them than the past. He who has loved you
and pardoned you shall never cease to love and pardon. He is alpha, and
He shall be omega, also. He is first, and He shall be last. When you shall
stand in the cold floods of Jordan, you need not fear because death cannot
separate you from His love. Now, soul, is not your love refreshed? Does
not this make you love Jesus? Does not a flight through limitless plains of
His love inflame your heart and compel you to delight yourself in the Lord
your God? Surely as we meditate on the love of the Lord, our hearts burn
within us, and we long to love Him more.

Charles Haddon Spurgeon

October 23—Love for Eternity

"Those who love their life lose it, and those who hate their life
in this world will keep it for eternal life." John 12:25 NRSV

*I*n souls filled with love, the desire to please God is a continual prayer.
As the furious hate that the devil bears us is termed the roaring of a lion,
so our vehement love may be termed crying after God. God only requires
that our hearts be truly purified and that we offer Him continually the
wishes and vows that naturally spring from perfect love.

We should be continually laboring to cut off all the useless things that
surround us. The best means of resisting the devil is to destroy whatever of
the world remains in us. In that way we can raise for God, upon its ruins,
a building all of love. Then shall we begin in this fleeting life to love God,
as we shall love Him in eternity.

John Wesley

And I ask him that with both feet planted firmly on love, you'll be able to take in with all Christians the extravagant dimensions of Christ's love. Ephesians 3:17–18 TM

I sometimes think we give a totally different meaning to the word "love" when it is associated with God. We well understand in its human application. Put together all the tenderest love you know of, the deepest you have ever felt, and the strongest that has ever been poured out upon you, then multiply it by infinity, and you will begin to have some faint glimpses of what the love of God in Christ Jesus is. And this is grace.

To be planted in grace is to live in the very heart of this love, to be enveloped by it, to be steeped in it, to revel in it, to know nothing else but love only and love always, and to have no shadow of a doubt but that it will surely order all things well. It is to be so satisfied with His skill and wisdom that not a question will cross our minds as to His modes of treatment. It is to grow as the lilies grow without a care and without anxiety, to grow because we live and therefore must grow, to grow because He who has planted has made us to grow.

Hannah Whitall Smith

ASSURED LOVE—OCTOBER 25

To those who have been called. . .Mercy, peace and love be yours in abundance. Jude 1–2 NIV

*W*hen I recall a prominent Christian friend, I am conscious of the sweet and gracious perfume that was ever rising from his full and ever-moving life. I like this sentence of his: "What a thrill it gives me to meet with one who has fallen in love with Jesus!" Yes, that is the speech of a lover who is himself in love with the Lord. It is the thrill of sympathetic vibrations. It is the thrill of one who is already in love with Jesus and who delights to see Jesus come to His own. This renowned Christian's sort of warfare finds its explanation in the lover's thrill—and in a lover's thrill has its secret in the lover's tranquility.

But why should I keep upon these high planes of renowned and prominent personalities? Get a person who is restfully intimate with his Lord, and you have a person whose force is tremendous! Such people move in apparent ease, but it is the ease that is linked with the infinite; it is the very peace of God. They may be engaged in apparent trifles, but even in the doing of the trifles there emerges the health-giving currents of the kingdom of God.

John Henry Jowett

OCTOBER 26—LOVE AND THE CHILD OF GOD

My little children, let us not love in word, neither in tongue;
but in deed and in truth. 1 John 3:18 KJV

*S*uppose you go and watch workmen at their task. The majority do their work in an uninterested, mechanical sort of way. They come exactly at the hour in the morning and throw down their work to a second exactly when the closing bell has rung. Perhaps you observe an uncomfortable turning of the head occasionally as if some eye were upon them, then a dogged going on of their work again as if it were always done under some restraint.

But among the workmen you notice one with cheerfulness about him. You see him at his place sometimes even before the bell has rung, and if unfinished work is in his hands when closing time has come, he does not mind an extra five minutes when all the others are gone.

Now the difference between them is this. The first set of men are hired workmen. The man by himself is the owner's son. They work for wages and keep the workshop laws in terror of losing their place. But the son keeps them, and keeps them better, not for wages but for love.

So the Christian keeps the will or the laws of God because of the love of God. Not because they are regulations framed and hung up before him at every moment of his life, but because they are his Master's will.

Henry Drummond

OCTOBER 27—THE PHYSICIAN'S LOVE

For the LORD corrects those he loves, just as a father corrects a child in whom he delights.
Proverbs 3:12 NLT

*W*hat a gross mistake it is to conclude that wrath must be in the Deity because He chastens. You have God's own Word for it that nothing but His love disciplines. How is it possible for words to give stronger proof that God is pure love, that he has no will toward fallen man but to bless him with works of love? What can infinite love do to give greater proof that all that it does proceeds from love?

To say "If God is all love toward fallen man, how can He threaten or chastise sinners?" is as absurd as to say "If the able physician is all love, goodness, and goodwill toward his patients, how can he apply painful remedies?" So absurd is this reasoning that the very lack of this chastisement would be the greatest of all proof that God was not all love and goodness toward man.

William Law

I. . .will deliver them out of all places where they have been scattered. . . . I will bring them. . .to their own land. . . . I will feed them in a good pasture. Ezekiel 34:12–14 KJV

The Good Shepherd searches the "far country" for His lost sheep. "I will bring them. . .out of all places where they have been scattered." He goes into the hard wilderness of cold indifference, and wasteful pride, and desolating sin, searching "high and low" for His foolish sheep. And no place is unvisited by the Great Seeker! Every perilous ravine, where a sheep can be lost, knows the footprints of the Shepherd.

And the Good Shepherd brings His wandering sheep back home. "I will bring them. . .to their own land." We return from the land of pride to the home of lowliness, from hard indifference to gracious sympathy, from the barrenness of sin to the beauty of holiness. We come back to God's beautiful "lily-land" of eternal light and peace.

And what nutriment the Good Shepherd provides for the homecoming sheep! "I will feed them in a good pasture." Our wasted powers shall be renewed and strengthened by the fattening diet of grace. Love shall be both host and meat! "He will satisfy thy mouth with good things."

John Henry Jowett

GROW IN LOVE—OCTOBER 29

Let them give thanks to the LORD for his unfailing love and his wonderful deeds for men, for he satisfies the thirsty and fills the hungry with good things. Psalm 107:8–9 NIV

Let me exhort Christians to increase your love to God. Let your love be raised up higher. Our love to God should be as the light of the morning: First there is the daybreak, then it shines brighter at noon.

When I see the almond tree bud and flourish, I know there is life in the root. Where we see love to God increasing and growing larger, we may conclude it is true and genuine. The disciples' love to Christ at first was weak; they fled from Christ. But after Christ's death, love grew more vigorous, and the disciples made an open declaration of Him.

If our love to God does not increase, it will soon decrease. If the fire is not stoked, it will quickly go out. Therefore Christians should above all things endeavor to cherish and excite their love to God. This encouragement will be out of date when we come to heaven, for then our light shall be clear and our love perfect; but now it is time to motivate ourselves so that our love to God may increase yet more and more.

Thomas Watson

OCTOBER 30—LOVE WRITTEN ON OUR HEARTS

"I will put my laws in their minds and write them on their hearts." Hebrews 8:10 NIV

*S*ervice can become bondage if it is done purely as a matter of duty. Instead of saying the "May I" of love, the soul finds itself saying the "Must I" of duty. One dear Christian expressed it to me this way. "When I was first converted," she said, "I was so full of joy and love that I was only too glad to do anything for my Lord. But after a while, my joy faded away and my love burned less fervently. I found myself involved in lines of service that were gradually becoming burdensome to me."

Or if this does not describe your case, perhaps another picture will. You do love your work in the abstract. But in doing it, you find so many responsibilities connected with it and so many doubts as to your own capacity that it becomes a very heavy burden. You have known this was the wrong way to feel and have been ashamed of it, but you have seen no way to help it. You have not loved your work.

If a man's will is really set on a thing, he regards with a sublime indifference the obstacles that lie in the way of his reaching it. What we need in the Christian life is to want to do God's will as much as other people want to do their own will. And this is what God has promised. He says He will write His laws on our hearts. We shall love His law because anything written on our hearts we must love.

Hannah Whitall Smith

OCTOBER 31—LOVE THAT ENABLES LOVE

For this is the message that ye heard from the beginning, that we should love one another.
1 John 3:11 KJV

*L*ove to others arises from the love of the Father. Do not attempt, then, to fulfill the commandment of brotherly love by yourselves. You are not in a position to do this. But believe that the Holy Spirit who is in you to make known the love of God to you also certainly enables you to produce this love. Never say, "I feel no love; I do not feel as if I can forgive this man." Feeling is not the rule of your duty but the command and the faith that God gives power to obey the command. In obedience to the Father, with the choice of your will and in faith that the Holy Spirit gives you power, begin to say, "I will love him; I do love him." The feeling will follow the faith. Let your love be a helpful, self-sacrificing love like that of Jesus.

Andrew Murray

They will betray their friends, be reckless, be puffed up with pride,
and love pleasure rather than God. 2 Timothy 3:4 NLT

A father's love to a wayward child is as sincere as his love to his obedient child at home, though it is a different kind. God cannot love you as a believer until you are such. But He loves you as a sinner. And it is this love of His to the unloving and unlovable that affords the sinner his first resting place. Herein is love: not that we loved God, but that He loved us.

"I am not satisfied with my repentance," you say. It is well. What should you have thought of yourself had you been satisfied? What pride and self-righteousness would it indicate if you said, "I am satisfied with my repentance—it is of the proper quality and amount." If satisfied with it, what would you do with it? Would you base your peace upon it? Would you pacify your conscience with it? Would you go with it instead of the blood to a holy God? If not, what do you mean by the desire to be satisfied with your repentance before having peace with God?

Horatius Bonar

THE LOVE OF OLD—NOVEMBER 2

In his love and mercy he redeemed them; he lifted them up and
carried them all the days of old. Isaiah 63:9 NIV

W e are all prone to think that the earliest days were the best. It is quite possible they were. But we must carefully distinguish between the exchange of the freshness and novelty of our first love for a deepening and maturing love. We should not reckon our position in God's sight by our raptures and count ourselves going backward because they have gone. There is something better than rapture—the peace of a settled understanding and unvarying faith.

Still, if you have left the old place at the feet of Christ and your love is cooling and your spirituality waning, I beseech you: Go back! Remember from what place you have fallen, repent, and do the first works. Jesus yearns to reinstate you. He has permitted this restless longing for the past to come that it may be with you as in the months of old. His lamp shall shine above your head again. The secret of the Lord shall be upon your tent; your steps shall be washed with butter and the rock pour out rivers of oil. Your roots shall spread to the waters, and the dew shall lie all night upon your branch.

F. B. Meyer

November 3—Personal Responsibility

For the Son of man is come to seek and to save that which was lost. Luke 19:10 KJV

I have often thought that the reason why so many pray only in form and not in heart for the salvation of souls is that they lack love like God's love for the souls of the perishing. They lack a sense of personal responsibility for the lost.

You must see impressively that souls are precious. Without such a sense of the value of souls, you will not pray with fervent, strong desire. Without a just apprehension of their guilt, danger, and remedy, you will not pray in faith for God's interposing grace.

You need so to love the world that your love will draw you to make similar sacrifices and put forth similar labors. Love for souls, the same in kind as God had in giving up His Son to die and as Christ had in coming cheerfully down to make Himself the offering, each servant of God must have. Otherwise, your prayers will have little heart and no power with God. This love for souls is always implied in acceptable prayer, that God would send forth laborers into His harvest.

Charles Finney

November 4—Seek Love

And hope does not disappoint us, because God's love has been poured into our hearts through the Holy Spirit that has been given to us. Romans 5:5 NRSV

Has our daily habit been to seek being filled with the Holy Spirit as the Spirit of love?

When the body is divided, there cannot be strength. In the time of great conflicts, one of the mottoes is: "Unity gives strength." It is only when God's people stand as one body, one before God in the fellowship of love, one toward another in deep affection, one before the world in love—it is only then that they will have power to secure the blessing which they ask of God. Remember, if a jar that ought to be one whole is cracked into many pieces, it cannot be filled. You can take a part of a jar and dip out a little water into that, but if you want the container full, it must be whole. Give yourselves up to love, and the Holy Spirit will come. Receive the Spirit, and He will teach you to love more.

Andrew Murray

A wise child loves discipline, but a scoffer does not listen to rebuke. Proverbs 13:1 NRSV

As soon as a man begins to live wisely and flees all the lusts, desires, and vanities, which he before was used to and loved, and bows himself under the yoke of God's holy doctrine; then his enemies begin to contrive by wiles, frauds, and temptations to make him fall. Therefore, his horse needs to be submissive and help his master to overcome his enemies. If the soul and the body are well-agreed and help one another in this spiritual contest, the devil shall soon flee and be overcome.

This is the right spur that should quicken your horse to speed in its way—that you learn to love Jesus Christ in all your living. This love would move such a person to live more virtuously and to flee from sin a hundred times more than any dread of the pain of hell. For perfect love puts out all dread and cleanses the soul from filth and makes it to see God and to flee often to heaven in its desires, hoping to dwell there forever.

John Wycliffe

SIN AGAINST LOVE—NOVEMBER 6

But you, O LORD, are a God merciful and gracious, slow to anger and abounding in steadfast love and faithfulness. Psalm 86:15 NRSV

A peculiarity of the sin of temper is that its worst influence is upon others. It is generally the weak who are the sufferers because temper is the prerogative of superiors. Subordinates have not only to bear the brunt of the storm, but to sink their own judgment and spend their lives in ministering to what they know to be caprice. When the young are disciplined by the iron instead of by the Golden Rule, the consequences are still more fatal. They feel that they do not get a fair hearing.

In its ultimate nature, bad temper is a sin against love. And however impossible it may be to realize that now, however we may condone it as a pardonable weakness or small infirmity, a sin against love is a sin against God, for God is love. He who sins against love sins against God.

Henry Drummond

Let the morning bring me word of your unfailing love, for I have put my trust in
you. Show me the way I should go, for to you I lift up my soul. Psalm 143:8 NIV

When a patient believes in a physician, he carefully follows his prescriptions and directions. There is no physician like Jesus. We put ourselves into His hands, accept whatever He prescribes, and do whatever He bids. We feel that nothing can be wrongly ordered while Jesus is the director of our affairs. He loves us too well to let us perish or suffer a single needless pain.

When a traveler trusts a guide to conduct him over a difficult pass, he follows the track that his guide points out. We trust Jesus to save us. He gives us directions as to the way of salvation. We follow those directions and are saved. Let not my reader forget this. Trust Jesus, and prove your trust by doing whatever He bids you.

Faith has the power of working by love. It influences the affections toward God and draws the heart after the best things. He who believes in God will beyond all question love God. Faith is an act of the understanding. To love God and to love man is to be conformed to the image of Christ.

Charles Haddon Spurgeon

NOVEMBER 8—LOVE DRIVES OUT SIN

Blessed is the man who perseveres under trial, because when he has stood the test, he will
receive the crown of life that God has promised to those who love him. James 1:12 NIV

Love to God will never let sin thrive in the heart.

The eye has seen rare sights; the ear has heard sweet music. But the eye has not seen, nor ear heard, nor can the heart of man conceive what God has prepared for them who love Him! Such glorious rewards are laid up that, as Augustine says, faith itself is not able to comprehend. God has promised a crown of life to them who love Him. This crown encircles within it all blessedness, riches, glory, and delight. It is a crown that fades not away.

Love to God is armor of proof against error. For want of hearts full of love, people have heads full of error; unholy opinions are for want of holy affections. People given up to strong delusions because they receive not the love of truth. The more we love God, the more we hate those opinions that would draw us off from God.

Thomas Watson

Rather, the LORD's delight is in those who honor him, those who
put their hope in his unfailing love. Psalm 147:11 NLT

We seemed to be reminded of the delight often taken by bride and bridegroom in spreading out for inspection the love gifts of their friends so that as many as possible may share their gratification in them. Several may have sent similar gifts, but each is set out to the best possible advantage with the name of the giver attached. And while the intrinsic value of each is not lost sight of, it is the expression of the loving thought that is most prized.

Again we were reminded of our frequent absence from home and children. Wifely letters have cheered and interested us, depicting with motherly tenderness the gifts the children had brought her on her birthday or other occasion. The letters have a fullness of detail that showed alike the pleasure of the writer and her consciousness of the enjoyment with which the account would be read.

God delights in the offering of His servants. He would say, "Behold the love gifts of My people! How many and how precious the offerings of each, and how great the value of the whole!"

Hudson Taylor

GIFTS OF LOVE—NOVEMBER 10

How great is the love the Father has lavished on us, that we should be called children of God!
1 John 3:1 NIV

God shows His love by His gifts. Suppose on his coronation day, King Edward, after all the ceremonies were over, had taken his carriage and had ridden down to the East End of London and had seen some ragged, wretched boy. Suppose his great heart of love had gone out to that boy, and stepping up to that poor wanderer, he had said: "I love you, and I am going to take you in my carriage to the palace. I am going to dress you fit to be a king's son, and you shall be known as the son of King Edward the Seventh." Would it not have been wonderful? But it would not have been as wonderful as that the infinitely holy God should have looked down upon you and me in our filthiness and rags and depravity and. . .have so loved us that He should have bestowed upon us to be called the sons of God.

Reuben Archer Torrey

And walk in love, as Christ also hath loved us, and hath given himself
for us an offering and a sacrifice to God for a sweetsmelling savour. Ephesians 5:2 KJV

A man was set to watch a railway drawbridge over a river. He threw it open and let vessels through. He heard the whistle of a train up the track and sprang to the lever to bring the bridge back into place. As he was doing so, he accidentally pushed his boy into the river. He heard the boy cry, "Father, save me; I am drowning." What should he do? The man stood at the post of duty and brought the bridge back so that the train could pass over in safety. Then he jumped into the river to save his boy, but it was too late. He sacrificed his boy to do his duty.

That man owed it to those on the train to do what he did. God owed you and me nothing. We were guilty rebels against Him.

What are you going to do with His love? Accept it, or trample it underfoot? Accept Christ, and you accept that love. Reject Christ, and you trample that love underfoot. I cannot understand how any man or woman in their right senses can harden their hearts against the love of God.

Reuben Archer Torrey

NOVEMBER 12—LOVE OF ELDERS

"Honor your father and your mother, so that you may live long in the
land the LORD your God is giving you." Exodus 20:12 NIV

*L*et your mind go back to the time when you were ill. Did your mother neglect you? A neighbor came in and said, "Now, Mother, you go and lie down. You have been up for a week. I will take your place for a night." Did your mother do it? No. If the poor worn body forced her to it at last, she lay watching. She would gladly have taken the disease into her own body to save you. No matter to what depths of vice and misery you have sunk, she has not turned you out of her heart. She would draw you back by the bands of a love that never dies.

When I was in England, I read of a man who professed to be a Christian, who was brought before the magistrate for not supporting his aged father. My friends, I'd rather be content with a crust of bread and a drink of water than neglect my father or mother. The idea that a professing Christian would neglect a parent! God have mercy on such a godless Christianity as that! It is a withered-up thing. Don't profess to love God and do a thing like that.

Dwight Lyman Moody

"He is so good! His faithful love endures forever!" 2 Chronicles 7:3 NLT

*L*et us thank God, then, that the consuming fire of His love will not cease to burn until it has refined us as silver is refined. For the promise is that He shall sit as a refiner and purifier of silver, and He shall purge us as gold and silver are purged in order that we may offer unto Him an offering in righteousness. He gives us this inspiring assurance that if we will but submit to this purifying process, we shall become pleasant unto the Lord and all nations shall call us blessed.

To be pleasant to the Lord may seem to us impossible when we look at our shortcomings and our unworthiness. But when we think of this lovely, consuming fire of God's love, we can be of good heart and take courage. He will not fail nor be discouraged until all our impurities are burned up and we ourselves come forth in His likeness and are tailored to His image.

Hannah Whitall Smith

LOVE CONQUERS SELFISHNESS—NOVEMBER 14

For God did not give us a spirit of timidity, but a spirit of power, of love and of self-discipline. 2 Timothy 1:7 NIV

*N*othing but love can expel and conquer our selfishness. Self is the great curse, whether in its relationship to God or to our fellowmen or to fellow Christians. But, praise God, Christ came to redeem us from self. Deliverance from selfishness means to be a vessel overflowing with love to everybody all the day. Many people pray for the power of the Holy Spirit, and they get something but so little! They prayed for power for work and power for blessing, but they have not prayed for power for full deliverance from self. A great many of us try hard at times to love. We try to force ourselves to love, and I do not say that is wrong; it is better than nothing. But the end of it is always very sad. "I fail continually," one must confess.

And how can I learn to love? Never until the Spirit of God fills my heart with God's love, and I begin to long for God's love in a very different sense from which I have sought it so selfishly as a comfort, a joy, a happiness, and a pleasure to myself.

Andrew Murray

NOVEMBER 15—LOVE AND CHRISTIAN PERFECTION

Therefore, as God's chosen people, holy and dearly loved, clothe yourselves with compassion, kindness, humility, gentleness and patience. Colossians 3:12 NIV

The person who strives for Christian perfection is holy both in heart and in all manner of conversation. He loves the Lord his God with all his heart and serves God with all his strength. He loves his neighbor; that is, every person as himself, yes, in the same way as Christ loves us. Indeed, his soul is all love and filled with mercy, kindness, meekness, gentleness, and longsuffering. And his life is full of the work of faith, the patience of hope, and the labor of love. Whatever he does either in word or deed, he does it all in the name—in the love and power—of the Lord Jesus. In a word, he does the will of God on earth as it is done in heaven.

This it is to be a perfect man, to have a heart so all-flaming with the love of God as continually to offer up every thought, word, and work as a spiritual sacrifice acceptable to God through Christ.

John Wesley

NOVEMBER 16—LOVE AND THE FACE OF JESUS

Jesus Christ. . .who loves us and has freed us from our sins by his blood. Revelation 1:5 NIV

A man's whole religion depends on his conception of God, so much so that to give a man religion in many cases is simply to correct his conception of God. But if man's natural conception of God is of a being opposed to him, a being to be appeased, his religion will be a religion of fear. God therefore was a God to be feared, an uncomfortable presence in one's life. He was always in court either actually sitting in judgment or collecting material for the next case.

The repetition that God was love did nothing to dispel this terrible illusion. We cannot love God because we are told to love Him, for love is not made to order. We can believe God's love, but believing love is like looking at heat. We cannot respond to it. To excite love, we need a person, not a doctrine—a father, not a deity. To be changed into the same image we must look at the glory of God in the face of Jesus. The old zealous preaching was defective in not exhibiting God in the face of Jesus.

Henry Drummond

Brethren, I write no new commandment unto you, but an old commandment which ye had from the beginning.... Again, a new commandment I write unto you ...because the darkness is past, and the true light now shineth. 1 John 2: 7–9 KJV

What a magic difference love makes to a face. It at once becomes a face illumined. Love makes the plainest face winsome and attractive. It adds to the light of heaven, and the earthly is transfigured. No cosmetics are needed when love is in possession. She will do her own beautifying work, and everybody will know her sign.

What a magic difference love makes in service! The hireling goes about his work with heavy and reluctant feet: the lover sings and dances at his toil. The hireling scamps his work: the lover is always adding another touch, and is never satisfied. Just one more touch! And just another! And so on until the good God shall say that loving "patience has had her perfect work."

Love lights up everything, for she is the light of life. Let her dwell in the soul, and every room in the life shall be filled with the glory of the Lord.

John Henry Jowett

IMITATE THE LOVE OF JESUS—NOVEMBER 18

Do not imitate what is evil but what is good. 3 John 11 NIV

As a husband, the Christian is to look upon the portrait of Christ Jesus, and he is to paint according to that copy. The true Christian is to be such a husband as Christ was to His church. The Lord Jesus cherishes for the church a special affection, which is set upon her above the rest of mankind. A husband should love his wife with a constant love, for this is the way that Jesus loves His church. He does not vary in His affection. He may change in His display of affection, but the affection itself is still the same. A husband should love his wife with an enduring love, for nothing shall be able to separate us from the love of God, which is in Christ Jesus our Lord. A true husband loves his wife with a hearty love, fervent and intense. It is not mere lip service. Jesus has a delighted love toward His spouse: He prizes her affection and delights in her with sweet contentment. Believer, you wonder at Jesus' love; you admire it—are you imitating it? In your domestic relationships, is the rule and measure of your love even as Christ loved the church?

Charles Haddon Spurgeon

He has taken me to the banquet hall, and his banner over me is love. Song of Songs 2:4 NIV

*I*was visiting once in a wealthy house, where there was an adopted girl upon whom was lavished all the love and tenderness and care that human hearts could give. And as I watched that child running about, free and lighthearted with the happy carelessness of childhood, I thought what a picture it was of our wonderful position as children in the house of our heavenly Father. And I said to myself, Nothing could so grieve and wound the loving hearts around her as to see this little child beginning to be worried or anxious about herself in any way, about whether her food and clothes would be provided for her, or how she was to get her education or her future support. How much more must the great, loving heart of our God and Father be grieved and wounded at seeing His children taking so much anxious care and thought! And I understood why it was that our Lord had said to us so emphatically, "Take no thought for yourselves."

Let the ways of childish confidence and freedom from care, which so please you and win your hearts in your own little ones, teach you what should be your ways with God.

Hannah Whitall Smith

NOVEMBER 20—THE PERFECTING OF LOVE

"Herein is our love made perfect." 1 John 4:11–21

*H*ow? By dwelling in God and God in us. Love is not a manufacture; it is a fruit. It is not born of certain works; it springs out of certain relations. It does not come from doing something; it comes from living with Somebody. "Abide in Me."

How many people are striving who are not abiding? They live in a manufactory, they do not live in a home. "This is life, to know Thee." When I am related to the Lord Jesus, when I dwell with Him, love is as surely born as beauty and fragrance are born when my garden and the springtime dwell together. If we would only wisely cultivate the fellowship of Jesus, everything else would follow in its train—all that gracious succession of beautiful things which are called "the fruits of the Spirit."

And "herein is our love made perfect." It is always growing richer, because it is always drawing riches from the inexhaustible love of God. "Our life is hid with Christ in God," and hence our love will "grow in all wisdom and discernment."

John Henry Jowett

...for with their mouth they shew much love, but their heart goeth after their covetousness.
Ezekiel 33:31 KJV

*B*y seven signs a man may suppose that he has the love of Christ. First, when all coveting of earthly things and fleshly lusts are weakened by Him. For where coveting is, there is not the love of Christ. The second is a burning desire for heaven. For when he has felt anything of heaven, the more he wants. The third sign is if his language has changed. He who used to speak of earth now speaks of heaven. The fourth sign is practicing what is for spiritual good—as when a person, leaving all other things, has good will and devotion to prayer and finds sweetness in doing so. The fifth is when things which are hard in themselves are made easy through love. The sixth is hardness of soul to suffer all anguishes and troubles. He has no joy but in God. He fears nothing except to offend God. And all his hope is to come from God.

The seventh sign is joyfulness when he is in tribulation and that he thanks Him in all afflictions that he suffers. It is the greatest token that he has the love of God: No tribulation or persecution can bring him down from this love.

John Wycliffe

LOVE WITHOUT BONDAGE—NOVEMBER 22

But it was because the LORD loved you. . .that he. . .redeemed you from the land of slavery.
Deuteronomy 7:8 NIV

*E*very sinner sees plainly that God must have good reason to be displeased with him. The selfish sinner judges God from himself. Knowing how he should feel toward one who had wronged him, he unconsciously infers that God must feel the same way toward every sinner. When he tries to pray, his heart won't; it is nothing but terror. He feels no attraction toward God, no real love.

God would lead us to serve Him in love and not in bondage. He would draw us forth into the liberty of the sons of God. He loves to see the obedience of the heart. He would inspire love enough to make all our service free, cheerful, and full of joy. If you wish to make others love you, you must give them your love. In this way God commends His love toward us in order to win our hearts to Himself and get us ready and fit to dwell forever in His eternal home.

Charles Finney

NOVEMBER 23—LOVE OF SOULS

Timely advice is as lovely as golden apples
in a silver basket. Proverbs 25:11 NLT

Consider, my fellow Christians, that it was love for souls that brought the blessed Jesus down from the bosom of His Father. Surely souls must be of infinite worth, which made the Lamb of God to die so shameful a death.

And shall not this make you have a true value for souls? It is of the greatest worth. This, then, is the greatest charity when it comes from love to God and from love to souls. May this make you have so much regard for the value of souls as not to neglect all opportunities for the doing of them good. Therefore, let me earnestly beseech you both to consider the worth of immortal souls and let your love extend to them. By your advice and admonition, you may be an instrument in the hands of God in bringing souls to the Lord Jesus. Let me once more beseech each of you to act according to the circumstances of life, which God in His rich and free mercy has given you.

George Whitefield

NOVEMBER 24—PREPARATION FOR MEETING GOD

For these commands and this teaching are a lamp to light the way ahead of you.
The correction of discipline is the way to life. Proverbs 6:23 NLT

Sooner or later we find out that life is not a holiday but a discipline. Earlier or later we all discover that the world is not a playground. It is quite clear God means it for a school. The moment we forget that, the puzzle of life begins. We try to play in school; the Master does not mind that so much for He likes to see His children happy, but in our playing, we neglect our lessons. We do not see how much there is to learn. Because He loves us, He comes into the school sometimes and speaks to us. Sometimes the voice is like a startling thunderclap during a summer night. The discipline may seem far less than we deserve or even to our eye ten times more. But it is not measured by these—it is measured solely by God's love, measured solely that the scholar may be better educated when he arrives at his Father. The discipline of life is a preparation for meeting the heavenly Father.

Henry Drummond

Yet in all these things we are more than conquerors
through Him who loved us. Romans 8:37 NKJV

My debt of love continually increases! Shall I dare to think of recompensing all Your love with mine? Will my mite compensate You for Your golden mines? Shall I dare to compete in love with You? Dare I set my faint spark against the sun of Your love? Can I love as high, deep, broad, and long as the one who is love Himself? As I cannot match You in the works of power, no more can I match You in love. No, Lord, I yield; I am overcome. When You lead me in triumph from earth to heaven, all who see it shall acknowledge that You have prevailed.

The Lord shall take my body from the grave and make me shine as the sun in glory forever and ever. Is not heaven the place for a meeting of lovers? Is not the life there a state of love? Is not the employment there the work of love where the souls with Christ will take their fill? My soul begins it here. Keep me now in the love of God, and let nothing separate me from it.

Richard Baxter

SACRIFICIAL LOVE—NOVEMBER 26

"You cannot serve God and wealth." Matthew 6:24 NRSV

If a man gives all his wealth, it is nothing. If he does great penance, it is little. If he gains all knowledge, he is still far afield. If he has great virtue and much ardent devotion, he still lacks a great deal and especially the one thing that is most necessary to him. What is this one thing? That is leaving all. He must forsake himself—completely renounce himself—and give up all personal desires. Then when he has done all that he knows ought to be done, let him consider it as nothing. Let him make little of what may be considered great. Let him in all honesty call himself an unprofitable servant.

No one, however, is more wealthy than such a man. No one is more powerful. No one freer than he who knows how to leave all things and think of himself as the least of all.

Thomas à Kempis

The steadfast love of the LORD never ceases, his mercies never come to an end.
Lamentations 3:22 NRSV

*T*ruly beyond the power of words is the sweetness of contemplation You give to those who love You. You have shown to me the sweetness of Your charity, especially in having made me when I did not exist, in having brought me back to serve You when I had gone far astray from You, in having commanded me to love You.

O fountain of unceasing love, what shall I say of You? How can I forget You who has been pleased to remember me even after I had wasted away and perished? You have shown mercy to Your servant beyond all hope and have exhibited grace and friendship beyond his deserving.

It is a great honor and a great glory to serve You and to despise all things for Your sake. They who give themselves gladly to Your most holy service will possess great grace. They who cast aside all carnal delights for Your love will find the most sweet consolation of the Holy Spirit. They who enter upon the narrow way for Your name and cast aside all worldly care will attain great freedom of mind.

Thomas à Kempis

November 28—Love Crucified

"It is no longer I who live, but Christ lives in me." Galatians 2:20 NKJV

*H*e who is a lover of God is dead to the world. He who is in love with God is not much in love with anything else. The love of God and ardent love of the world are inconsistent. Love to God swallows up all other love. When a man's heart is raised above the world in the admiring and loving of God, how poor and slender are these things on earth below!

Will God ever bestow heaven upon them who so basely undervalue Him, preferring glittering dust before the glorious Deity? What is there in the earth that we should so set our hearts upon it? The world has no real intrinsic worth; it is but paint and deception.

Thomas Watson

"If I but touch his clothes, I will be made well." Mark 5:27–28 NRSV

*T*he God of patience, meekness, and love is the one God of my heart. The whole bent and desire of my soul is to seek for all my salvation in and through the merits and mediation of the meek, humble, patient, resigned, suffering Lamb of God. He alone has power to bring forth the blessed birth of these heavenly virtues in my soul.

He is the bread of God who came down from heaven of which the soul must eat—or perish and pine in everlasting hunger. He is the eternal love and meekness who left the bosom of His Father to be Himself the resurrection of meekness and love in all the darkened, wrathful souls of fallen men.

What a comfort is it to think that this Lamb of God, Son of the Father, light of the world, glory of heaven, and joy of angels is as near to us—is truly in the presence of us—as He is in the presence of heaven. A desire of our heart that presses toward Him, longing to catch one small spark of His heavenly nature, is as sure of finding Him, touching Him, and drawing power from Him as the woman who was healed by longing but to touch the border of His garment.

William Law

Sympathetic Love—November 30

"In accordance with your great love, forgive the sin of these people, just as you have pardoned them from the time they left Egypt until now." Numbers 14:19 NIV

*G*od shows His love by pardoning sin. God tells us plainly in His Word that He is willing to forgive any sinner who lives, no matter how deep down he has gone, if he will only turn from sin and turn to God.

God shows His love for us by sympathizing with us. There is not a man or woman who is in trouble but God sympathizes with you. Some of you may know what it is to have a child sick for a long time. At first, friends came and sympathized with you, but their sympathy has grown cold. As you have watched day and night, you have said: "There is no one who sympathizes with me." Yes, there is. God sympathizes with you. There are men and women who have a sorrow of such a character that they cannot confide it to any human ear. They say: "Nobody knows it. Nobody sympathizes with me." Yes, there is One who knows, and He sympathizes with you—God.

Reuben Archer Torrey

"Be careful to obey all the commands I give you; show love to the LORD your God by walking in his ways and clinging to him." Deuteronomy 11:22 NLT

A great many people say that if they keep the commandments they do not need to be forgiven and saved through Christ. But have you kept them? Young lady, can you say, "I am ready to be weighed by the law"? Can you, young man? Face the Ten Commandments honestly and prayerfully. See if your life is right and if you are treating God fairly. Let us get alone with God and read His law—read it carefully and prayerfully, and ask Him to forgive us our sin and what He would have us to do.

Is your heart set upon God alone? Have you no other god? If we were true to the first commandment, then obedience to the remaining nine would follow naturally. It is because we are unsound in the first that we break the others.

Dwight Lyman Moody

December 2—Love and Obedience

"If you listen to these regulations and obey them faithfully, the LORD your God will keep his covenant of unfailing love with you." Deuteronomy 7:12 NLT

A Christian lady expressed to a friend how impossible she found it to say, "Thy will be done." She was the mother of a little boy. Her friend said, "Suppose little Charley came running to you and said, 'Mother, I know you love me, and I am going to trust myself to your love.' You say, 'Now I shall have a chance to make Charley miserable. I will take away all his pleasures and fill his life with every hard and disagreeable thing I can find. I will compel him to do just the things that are the most difficult for him to do and will give him all sorts of impossible commands.' Would you respond in that way?"

The indignant mother replied, "You know I would not. You know I would hug him to my heart and cover him with kisses—and fill his life with all that was sweet and best."

"And are you more loving than God?" asked her friend.

The Christian mother said, "I see my mistake, and I will not be afraid of saying 'Thy will be done' to my heavenly Father any more than I would want my Charley to be afraid of saying it to me."

Hannah Whitall Smith

May those who love your salvation repeatedly shout, "God is great!" Psalm 70:4 NLT

*D*o not be surprised if there should be matters in the Bible, in your own life, and in the secular government of the world that baffle your mind. Remember you are only a little child in a class for infants. It is not likely that you can comprehend the whole system of your instructor. God would cease to be God to us if we by searching could find Him out.

But though we cannot find out God by the searching of the intellect, we may know Him by love. "He who loves knows God; for God is Love." There is a way of knowing God which is hidden from the wise and prudent but revealed to babes. Seek to be strengthened with might by His Spirit in the inner person. Let Christ dwell deep in your heart by faith. Take care to obey all His commandments, and then the holy God will come into you. He will give you Himself, and you will know Him as a little child knows its parent, whom it cannot grasp with its mind but loves and trusts and knows with its heart. We cannot find out God by searching, but we can by loving.

We can also find Him in the character and life of Jesus. He who has seen Jesus has seen the Father; why, then, ask to be shown the Father?

F. B. Meyer

PRAYER AND LOVE—DECEMBER 4

Praise be to God, who has not rejected my prayer or withheld his love from me!
Psalm 66:20 NIV

*A*re we praying as Christ did? Are our pleas and spirit the overflow of His spirit and pleas? Does love rule the spirit—perfect love? As our great example in prayer, our Lord puts love as a primary condition—a love that has purified the heart from all the elements of hate, revenge, and ill will. Love is the supreme condition of prayer, a life inspired by love.

Answered prayer is the spring of love and is the direct encouragement to pray. A few short, feeble prayers have always been a sign of a low spiritual condition. People ought to pray much and apply themselves to it with energy and perseverance. Eminent Christians have been eminent in prayer. The deep things of God are learned nowhere else. Great things for God are done by great prayers. A person who prays much studies much, loves much, works much, and does much for God and humanity.

Edward McKendree Bounds

December 5—Governed by Love

But the aim of such instruction is love that comes from a pure heart. 1 Timothy 1:5 NRSV

I believe that a person filled with the love of God is still liable to involuntary transgressions. They are in no way contrary to love, nor therefore, in the scripture sense, sin. Such transgressions you may call sins if you please; I do not. Let those who do not call them sins never think that themselves or any other persons are in such a state as that they can stand before infinite justice without a mediator.

Many mistakes may consist with pure love. Some may accidentally flow from it. I mean, love itself may incline us to mistake. The pure love of our neighbor, springing from the love of God, thinks no evil and believes and hopes all things. Now this very unsuspicious mind, ready to believe and hope the best of all people, may cause us to think some people are better than they really are. Here then is a clearly apparent mistake accidentally flowing from pure love.

We can avoid setting perfection too high or too low by keeping to the Bible and setting it just as high as the scripture does. It is nothing higher and nothing lower than this—the pure love of God and man.

John Wesley

December 6—Love Beyond Reason

The LORD is slow to anger, abounding in love and forgiving sin and rebellion. Numbers 14:18 NIV

G od's love—how could we understand? God's forgiveness—how could we understand? We need not be distressed if we do not understand them. Most things in religion are matters of simple faith. But when we come to the atonement, we want to see through it and understand it—as if it were finite like ourselves, as if it could ever be compassed by our narrow minds—as if God did not know that we never could fathom it when He said "Believe it," instead of "Understand it."

We do not ask for a theory of love before we begin to love or a theory of prayer before we begin to pray. We just begin. When they brought the sick man once to Jesus, He just said, "Man, your sins are forgiven you," and the man just believed it. He did not ask, "But why should You forgive me?" The fact is, if we would come to Christ just now, we should never ask any questions. If you will not receive salvation as a fact, receive the Lord Jesus Christ as a gift.

Henry Drummond

But I pray to you, O LORD, in the time of your favor; in your great love, O God,
answer me with your sure salvation. Psalm 69:13 NIV

*A*lmighty God is the very highest model, and to be like Him is to possess the highest character. Prayer molds us into the image of God and at the same time tends to mold others into the same image just in proportion as we pray for others. Prayer means to be Godlike, and to be Godlike is to love Christ and love God, to be one with the Father and the Son in spirit, character, and conduct.

God has much to do with believing people who have a living, transforming faith in Jesus Christ. These are God's children. A father loves his children, supplies their needs, hears their cries, and answers their requests. A child believes his father, loves him, trusts in him, and asks him for what he needs, believing without doubting that his father will hear his requests. God has everything to do with answering the prayer of His children. Their troubles concern Him, and their prayers awaken Him. Their voice is sweet to Him. He loves to hear them pray, and He is never happier than to answer their prayers.

Edward McKendree Bounds

LOVING THE LORD—DECEMBER 8

And he answering said, Thou shalt love the LORD thy God with all thy heart, and with all
thy soul, and with all thy strength, and with all thy mind; and thy neighbour as thyself.
Luke 10:27 KJV

*L*ove is not a work, it is a fruit. It grows in suitable soils, and it is our part to prepare the soils. When the conditions are congenial, love appears, just as the crocus appears in the congenial air of the spring.

What, then, can we do? We can seek the Lord's society. We can think about Him...read about Him...fill our imaginations with the grace of His life and service. We can be much with Him, talking to Him in prayer, singing to Him in praise, telling Him our yearnings and confessing to Him our defeats. And love will be quietly born. For this is how love is born between heart and heart. Two people are "much together," and love is born! We are with One who already loves us with an everlasting love. We are with One who yearns for our love and who seeks in every way to win it. "We love Him because He first loved us." And when we truly love God, every other kind of holy love will follow. Given the fountain, the rivers are sure.

John Henry Jowett

DECEMBER 9—OBLIGATIONS OF LOVE

By this we know that we love the children of God, when we love
God, and keep his commandments. 1 John 5:2 KJV

Jesus loves you with more than the love of friendship. As a bridegroom rejoices over his bride, so does He rejoice over you. Have you never longed to lavish your love and attentions upon someone far-off from you in position or circumstances? Have you not felt a capacity for self-surrender and devotedness that has seemed to burn within you like a fire and yet had no object upon which it dared to lavish itself?

If, then, you are hearing the sweet voice of your Lord calling you to Himself, will you shrink or hesitate? No! You will spring out to meet His dear call with an eager joy. Even His slightest wish will become a binding law to you, which it would fairly break your heart to disobey.

The obligations of love will be to you its sweetest privileges. The perfect happiness of perfect obedience will dawn upon your soul, and you will begin to know something of what Jesus meant when He said, "I delight to do Your will, O My God." And do you think the joy will be all on your side? The Lord has joy in those who have surrendered themselves to Him and who love to obey Him.

Hannah Whitall Smith

DECEMBER 10—LOVE REVEALED

"I made your name known to them, and I will make it known, so that the love with
which you have loved me may be in them, and I in them." John 17:26 NRSV

The history of God's communication with men is the chronicle of His love. This will be our textbook forever. We can contemplate no more sublime and ennobling theme. The brightness of the material universe pales before the splendors of the divine character—that central fire which melts the hearts of sinners on earth.

In love revealed, there are ceaseless wonders. Our surprise is ever new when we discover that God so loves us that He gave His well-beloved Son to the humiliation of the manger, the agonies of Gethsemane, the mockery of the trial before Pilate, and the ignominy of Calvary. But this was but the beginning of His generosity. The loving Father has bestowed an abiding gift—the Holy Spirit—to whisper in the ear of spiritual death the words of life, to pardon penitence, and to fully restore the lost image of God.

Daniel Steele

Keep your lives free from the love of money,
and be content with what you have.
Hebrews 13:5 NRSV

*H*is book was nearly done now. He had not forgotten the question "Would Jesus do this?" Would He write this story? It was a social novel written in a style that had proved popular. It had no purpose except to amuse. Its moral teaching was not bad, but neither was it Christian in any positive way.

"What would Jesus do?" He felt that Jesus would never write such a book. The question intruded on him at the most inopportune times. He became irritable over it. The standard of Jesus for an author was too ideal. Of course Jesus would use His powers to produce something useful or helpful or with a purpose. What was he, Jasper Chase, writing this novel for? Why, what nearly every writer wrote for—money and fame as a writer. There was no secret with him that he was writing this new story with that object. But he was urged on by his desire for fame as much as anything.

He turned to his desk and began to write. When he had finished the last page of the last chapter of his book, it was nearly dark. "What would Jesus do?" He had finally answered the question by denying his Lord. It grew darker in his room. Jasper Chase grew into a cold, cynical, formal life, writing novels that were social successes, but each one with a sting in it, the reminder of his denial, the bitter remorse that, do what he would, no social success could remove.

Charles Sheldon

"For the Father loves the Son, and shows Him all things that He Himself does;
and He will show Him greater works than these, that you may marvel." John 5:20 NKJV

The man who loves God with all his heart is in a right state; the man who does not love Him in this way is in a wrong one. He is a sinner because his heart is not right with God. He may think his life a good one, and others may think the same. But the outward good cannot make up for the inward evil. The good deeds done for his fellowman cannot offset his bad thoughts of God. And he is full of these bad thoughts so long as he does not love the infinitely lovable and infinitely glorious God with all his strength.

However favorably a good outward life may dispose himself and others to look upon his case, the verdict will go against him. There is another and yet worse charge against him. That his heart is not right with God is the first charge against him. That his heart is not right with the Son of God is the second. And it is this second that is the crowning, crushing sin, carrying with it more terrible condemnation than all other sins together.

Horatius Bonar

December 13—The God of Comfort

Let your steadfast love become my comfort according to your
promise to your servant. Psalm 119:76 NRSV

Among all the names that reveal God, the "God of all comfort" seems to me one of the most absolutely comforting. The words "all comfort" admit of no limitation and no deductions. But it often seems that a large number of the children of God are full, not of comfort but of the utmost discomfort. This discomfort arises from anxiety as to their relationship to God and doubts as to His love. They torment themselves with the thought that they are too good-for-nothing to be worthy of His care, and they suspect Him of being indifferent to their trials and of forsaking them in times of need. They are anxious and troubled by their indifference to the Bible, lack of fervency in prayer, and coldness of heart. They are tormented with regrets over their past and with anxieties for their future.

Such Christians spread gloom and discomfort around them wherever they go. And the manifestly uncomfortable religious lives of so many Christians is, I am very much afraid, responsible for a large part of the unbelief of the world.

Hannah Whitall Smith

Bear in mind that our LORD's patience means salvation, just as our dear brother Paul also wrote you with the wisdom that God gave him. 2 Peter 3:15 NIV

God's love is a most patient love. How rare to find a parent so loving his child as never to be impatient. How many of you parents can say that you love all your children so well that you have never felt impatient toward any of them—so that you can take them in your arms under the greatest provocations and love them down, love them out of their sins, love them into repentance and into an obedient spirit? Of which of your children can you say, "Thank God, I never fretted against that child." Often have I heard parents say, "I love my children, but how my patience fails me!"

But God never frets. He is never impatient. His love is so deep and so great that He is always patient.

Sometimes when parents have unfortunate children—poor objects of compassion—they can bear with anything from them. But when they are very wicked, they seem to feel that they are quite excusable for being impatient. In God's case, these are not unfortunate children but are intensely wicked—intelligently wicked. But His amazing patience—so set upon their good, so desirous of their highest welfare—that however they abuse Him, He sets Himself to bless them still and weep them down and melt them into penitence and love by the death of His Son in their stead!

Charles Finney

LOVE AND MEEKNESS—DECEMBER 15

I learned God—worship when my pride was shattered. Heart-shattered lives ready for love don't for a moment escape God's notice. Psalm 51:17 TM

No person can attain any degree of true love to Jesus unless he is truly meek.

By two things principally may a man know whether he is meek: and if his heart is not moved though his own will be contradicted and criticized—and when he is despised, falsely accused, and slandered; and if his will stands unmoved, not desiring revenge, and his mouth be shut from answers that are not meek. For he who has entered truly into God's love is not grieved with whatever slander, shame, or reproof he suffers for the love of his Lord. He is glad that he is worthy to suffer pain for Christ's love. Christ's disciples went in joy when they were worthy to suffer wrongs for the name of Jesus.

John Wycliffe

December 16—Love's Expenditures

*Hereby perceive we the love of God, because he laid down his life for us:
and we ought to lay down our lives for the brethren. 1 John 3:16 KJV*

There is much spurious love about. It lays nothing down; it only takes things up! It is self-seeking, using the speech and accents of love. It is a "work of the flesh," which has stolen the label of a "fruit of the Spirit." Love may always be known by its expenditures, its self-crucifixions, its Calvarys. Love is always laying down its life for others. Its pathway is always a red road. You may track its goings by the red "marks of the Lord Jesus."

And this is the life, the love-life, which the Lord Jesus came to create among the children of men. It is His gracious purpose to form a spiritual fellowship in which every member will be lovingly concerned about his fellows' good. A real family of God would be one in which all the members bleed for each, and each for all.

How can we gain this disposition of love? "God is love." "We love because He first loved us." At the fountain of eternal love we, too, may become lovers, becoming "partakers of the divine nature," and filled with all "the fullness of God."

John Henry Jowett

December 17—Love—The Cure for Anger

*But when the kindness and love of God our Savior appeared. . .He saved us through
the washing of rebirth and renewal by the Holy Spirit. Titus 3:4–5 NIV*

Christianity professes to cure anything. The process may be slow, the discipline may be severe, but it can be done. But is not temper a constitutional thing? Is it not hereditary, a family failing, a matter of temperament, and can that be cured? Yes, if there is anything in Christianity. If there is no provision for cure, then Christianity stands convicted of being unequal to human need.

It is quite useless by force of will to seek to empty the angry passions out of our life. Who has not made a thousand resolutions in this direction, only and with unutterable regret to see them dashed to pieces with the first temptation? The soul is to be made sweet not by taking the acidulous fluids out but by putting something in—a great love, God's great love. This is to work a chemical change upon them, to renovate and regenerate them, to dissolve them in love's own rich, fragrant substance. If a man let this into his life, his cure is complete; if not, it is hopeless.

Henry Drummond

The LORD lift up his countenance upon thee, and give thee peace. Numbers 6:26 KJV

Considered as a father's blessing, could anything be more appropriate than "The Lord bless you and keep you"? Is not this just what every loving father seeks to do, to bless and keep his children? He does not find it an unwelcome task but his greatest delight.

Nor may we confine ourselves to paternal love in thinking of this subject. Rather take it as embracing also the love of the mother. We all know how the mother-love delights to lavish itself on the objects of its care. With a patience that never tires, an endurance almost inexhaustible, and a care all but unlimited, how often has the mother sacrificed her very life for the welfare of her babe. But strong as is a mother's love, it may fail. God's love never fails.

"Jehovah, the Father, bless you and keep you." It is an individual blessing, and it includes every form of blessing, temporal as well as spiritual. He wants us His children to know and to enjoy the love that is the source of all blessing, the love that can never by finite words express its fullness, the love that eternal ages will never exhaust!

Hudson Taylor

THE END OF THE LAW—DECEMBER 19

" 'Love the LORD your God with all your heart. . . .
Love your neighbor as yourself.' " Matthew 22:37, 39 NKJV

All the divine precepts are referred back to love. Every commandment harks back to love. Love in this context of course includes both the love of God and the love of our neighbor. Therefore whatsoever things God commands and whatsoever things are not positively ordered but are strongly advised as good spiritual counsel—all of these imperatives are rightly obeyed only when they are measured by the standard of our love of God and our love of our neighbor.

This applies both in the present age and in the world to come. Now we love God in faith; then, at sight. Love comes at last to that fullness which cannot be surpassed. Who, then, can explain how great the power of love will be when there will be no sinful desire for it to overcome? For then the supreme state of true health will have been reached when the struggle with death shall be no more.

Augustine

"What do you want me to do for you?" Jesus asked him. Mark 10:51 NIV

Virginia Page said, "I find it specially difficult to answer that question on account of my money. Our Lord never owned any property. What I am trying to discover is a principle that will enable me to come to the nearest possible to His action as it ought to influence the entire course of my life so far as my wealth and its use are concerned.

"I have been educated in one of the most expensive schools in America and launched into society as an heiress. I can do as I please. I can gratify almost any want or desire; and yet when I honestly try to imagine Jesus living the life I have lived and am expected to live, I am under condemnation for being one of the most wicked, selfish, useless creatures in all the world.

"Dear friends, I do not want any of you to credit me with an act of great generosity. I have come to know lately that the money which I have called my own is not mine, but God's. If I, as steward of His, see some wise way to invest His money, it is not an occasion for vainglory or thanks from anyone simply because I have proved in my administration of the funds He has asked me to use for His glory."

Virginia Page, one of the city's leading society heiresses, dedicated her entire fortune to the Christian daily paper and the work of reform in the slum district known as the Rectangle.

Charles Sheldon

For the LORD loves justice; he will not forsake his faithful ones. Psalm 37:28 NRSV

Alexander Powers said, "The company gives me the use of this room, and I am going to fit it up with tables and a coffeemaker in the corner. My plan is to provide a good place where the men can come and eat their lunch and to give them, two or three times a week, the privilege of a fifteen-minute talk on some subject that will be a real help to them in their lives. They are, as a whole, entirely removed from church influence.

"I asked, 'What would Jesus do?' Among other things it seemed to me He would begin to act in some way to add to the lives of these men more physical and spiritual comfort. It is a very little thing, this room and what it represents, but I acted on the first impulse, to do the first thing that appealed to my good sense."

Later certain papers had fallen into his hands of the violation of the Interstate Commerce Law. What business of his was it? But if he saw a man entering his neighbor's house to steal, would it not be his duty to inform the officers of the law? Was a railroad company such a different thing? Was it under a different rule of conduct, so that it could rob the public and defy law and be undisturbed because it was such a great organization?

Alexander Powers handed in his resignation and placed his evidence against the company in the hands of the commission, and it is now for them to take action upon it.

Charles Sheldon

DECEMBER 22—GOD'S LOVE IN CONVERTING SINNERS

For by grace are ye saved through faith; and that not of yourselves: it is the gift
of God: Not of works, lest any man should boast. Ephesians 2:8–9 KJV

There is no room for any man's boasting of his own abilities and power; or as though he had done anything that might deserve such immense favors from God. God Himself is the author of this great and happy change. Love is His inclination to do us good considered simply as creatures: Mercy respects us as apostate and miserable creatures. That love of God is great love, and that mercy of His is rich mercy. Every converted sinner is a saved sinner. The grace that saves them is the free, undeserved goodness and favor of God, and He saves them not by the works of the law, but through faith in Christ Jesus. Both that faith and that salvation are the gifts of God.

Matthew Henry

DECEMBER 23—THE TWO GREAT COMMANDMENTS

You shall love.... Mark 12:30 NASB

Loving the Lord God with all your heart, mind, soul, and strength is the first great branch of Christian righteousness. You shall delight yourself in the Lord your God; seeking and finding all happiness in Him. You shall hear and fulfill His word, "My son, give me your heart." And having given Him your inmost soul to reign there without a rival, you may well cry out in the fullness of your heart, "I will love You, O my Lord, my strength. The Lord is my strong rock; my Savior, my God, in whom I trust."

The second commandment, the second great branch of Christian righteousness, is closely and inseparably connected with the first: "Love your neighbor as yourself." Use the same unwearied care to screen them from whatever might grieve or hurt either their soul or body. This is love.

John Wesley

Shew thy marvellous lovingkindness. . . . Psalm 17:7 KJV

*W*hen we give our hearts with our alms, we give well, but we must often plead to a failure in this respect. Not so our Master and our Lord. His favours are always performed with the love of His heart. He does not send to us the cold meat and the broken pieces from the table of His luxury, but He dips our morsel in, His own dish and seasons our provisions with the spices of His fragrant affections. When He puts the golden tokens of His grace into our palms, He accompanies the gift with such a warm pressure of our hand that the manner of His giving is as precious as the boon itself. Beloved, with what smiles does He speak! What golden sentences drop from His gracious lips! What embraces of affection does He bestow upon us!

Charles Haddon Spurgeon

THE LOVE OF CHRISTMAS—DECEMBER 25

For God so loved the world, that he gave his only begotten Son, that whosoever believeth in him should not perish, but have everlasting life. John 3:16 KJV

*I*n order to redeem and save us, it pleased God to give his only begotten Son. He gave him—that is, he gave him up to suffer and die—for us. His enemies could not have taken him if his Father had not given him. By sacrificing his Son, God showed his love to the world. He loved the world so really, so richly. Behold, and wonder, that the great God should love such a worthless world, that the holy God should love such a wicked world. The Jews thought that the Messiah would be sent in love only to their nation, but Christ tells them that he came in love to the whole world, Gentiles as well as Jews. Through him there is a general offer of life and salvation for all. God loved the world so much that he sent his Son with this fair proposal: Whosoever believes in him shall not perish.

Matthew Henry

DECEMBER 26—GOD'S LOVE IS BETTER THAN WINE

For thy love is better than wine. Song of Solomon 1:2 KJV

*I*n this place, the word *love* means the continual proofs and tokens of His love, which are said to be better than wine. Wine is a figure of prosperity and of all good and desirable things. The wine from the grape exhilarates and gives strength, but it only strengthens for a time; while the love of Christ is better than all earthly good and gives divine strength that abides.

It is entering into deep communion with Him; it is lying at His feet during those moments that are spent alone with Him: it is the consciousness of being well-pleasing to Him and having His love upon us: it is the holy familiarity with which we pour out our own love at His feet, and tell Him all things concerning ourselves. It is at such times that our enraptured souls cry: "Thy love is better than wine!"

Cora Harris MacIlravy

DECEMBER 27—LOVE AND FRIENDSHIP

A friend loveth at all times. Proverbs 17:17 KJV

*F*riendship is a wondrous thing. The love of friendship is often stronger than the love of brotherhood and sisterhood. There is a cord of tenderness and appreciation binding those who are friends, which is lovely beyond words to express it.

A friendship does not grow up spontaneously. It must have a good soil in which to take root, good seed from which to start, and care and cultivation, in order to become its best. The good soil is sincerity and truth coupled with kindness and affection. The good seed is love and appreciation. And it must be watched closely that no weeds of jealousy or envy creep in; the soil must be constantly stirred by kind acts, words of appreciation and affection, and mutual admiration.

Mabel Hale

"Whoever loses his life for me will find it." Matthew 16:25 NIV

*C*onsider the cross lying in your path with all its circumstances. It has a quality specific to you. It is prepared by God for you. It is given by God to you. And He gives it to you as a token of His love. If you receive it as such, it is ordered by Him for your good. After using such means to remove the pressure as Christian wisdom directs, lie as clay in the potter's hand. It is for your good, both with regard to the quality of it, its quantity and degree, its duration, and every other circumstance.

In all this, we may easily conceive our blessed Lord to act as the Physician of our souls. He does not act for His pleasure merely, but for our profit, that we may be partakers of His holiness. If, in searching our wounds, He puts us to pain, it is only to heal them.

John Wesley

GOD'S LOVE MEANS JOY—DECEMBER 29

Thou wilt shew me the path of life: in thy presence is fullness of joy; at thy right hand there are pleasures for evermore. Psalm 16:11 KJV

*T*o the children of God, there is behind all that changes and can change, the one unchangeable joy that God is. And while He is, His children will be cared for, and they ought to know it and rejoice in it, as instinctively and far more intelligently than the child of human parents. For what else can God do, being what He is? Neglect, indifference, forgetfulness, ignorance are all impossible to Him. He knows everything, He cares about everything, He can manage everything, and He loves us! Surely this is enough for a "fullness of joy" beyond the power of words to express; no matter what else may be missed besides.

Hannah Whitall Smith

DECEMBER 30—LOVE POWERS PURPOSE

*That thou mayest love the LORD thy God, and that thou
mayest obey his voice. . . . Deuteronomy 30:20 KJV*

A purpose in life gives something to live for, something to work for, and something to hope for. If the purpose be for a good cause, then the evil that would hinder can be overcome and the good prevail. But without this strong purpose, the individual becomes but a creature of circumstances, a chip tossed by the waves of life.

The power of purpose is the power of love. No man can cleave to any purpose with all his heart unless he loves the cause for which he strives. Those who have made a success in anything have done so because they set about the task with purpose. They loved sincerely the cause for which they labored, and they gave it their attention in spite of all that came to hinder them.

Mabel Hale

DECEMBER 31—LOVE IN THE YEAR TO COME

Continue in prayer. Colossians 4:2 KJV

H ast thou no mercy to ask of God? Then may the Lord's mercy show thee thy misery! A prayerless soul is a Christless soul. Prayer is the lisping of the believing infant, the shout of the fighting believer, the requiem of the dying saint falling asleep in Jesus. It is the breath, the watchword, the comfort, the strength, the honour of a Christian. If thou be a child of God, thou wilt seek thy Father's face, and live in thy Father's love. Pray that this year thou mayst be holy, humble, zealous, and patient; have closer communion with Christ, and enter oftener into the banqueting-house of His love. Pray that thou mayst be an example and a blessing unto others—and that thou mayst live more to the glory of thy Master. The motto for this year must be, "Continue in prayer."

Charles Haddon Spurgeon

THE WAY TO JESUS CHRIST IS SIMPLE:

1. ADMIT THAT YOU ARE A SINNER.

For all have sinned, and come short
of the glory of God.
ROMANS 3:23

2. BELIEVE THAT JESUS IS GOD THE SON WHO PAID THE WAGES OF YOUR SIN.

For the wages of sin is death [eternal separation
from God]; but the gift of God is eternal life
through Jesus Christ our Lord.
ROMANS 6:23

3. CALL UPON GOD.

If thou shalt confess with thy mouth the Lord Jesus,
and shalt believe in thine heart that God hath raised him
from the dead, thou shalt be saved.
ROMANS 10:9

SALVATION IS A VERY PERSONAL THING BETWEEN YOU AND GOD. THE DECISION IS YOURS ALONE.